MY INSTANT POT RECIPES

2022

EASY AND BUDGET-FRIENDLY RECIPES

JAMES SMITH

Table of Contents

Hot Chicken Soup 9

Chicken Fillets with Bacon and Cheese 11

Mediterranean Chicken Wraps 13

Family Chicken Wings 15

Chicken Fillets with Cheese Dip 17

Mexican-Style Chicken Tacos 19

Southern Chicken Stew 22

Turkey Chowder with Swiss Chard 24

Instant Cheesy Chicken Drumsticks 26

Spicy Chicken Wingettes 28

Turkey Legs Delight 30

Old-Fashioned Paprikash 31

Medley with Chicken and Mushrooms 33

Instant Chicken Teriyaki 35

Lazy Chicken Carnitas 37

Tasty Chicken Goulash 39

Turkey Meatloaf with Parmigiano-Reggiano 41

Southern Turkey Soup 43

Thai-Style Chicken 45

Chicken Thighs with Green Beans and Potatoes 47

Quick and Easy Garlic Shredded Chicken 49

The Ultimate Mexican Chicken 51

Instant Rotisserie Chicken 53

Turkey with Leeks and Mushrooms 55

Chicken with Onion and Green Olives 57

Juicy and Fall-off-Bone Drumsticks 59

Slow-Cooked Turkey 61

Mediterranean Chicken Wings 63

Green Chicken 65

Juicy Herbed Turkey Breasts 67

Chicken Spaghetti Squash with Shitakes 69

Thai Peanut Chicken 71

Thai Goose with Basil 73

Coconut Kale Chicken 75

Instant Pot Garlic Chicken 77

Instant Pot Lemon Olive Chicken 78

Instant Pot Chicken Shawarma 80

Italian-Inspired Creamy Chicken 82

Instant Pot Pesto Chicken 84

Lemon Chicken 85

Delicious Beef Stew 87

Classic Lamb Leg 88

Asian Pork 90

Salsa Pork 92

BBQ Pork Ribs	94
BBQ Pulled Pork	96
Pork Chops with Gravy	98
Spicy & Smoky Beef	100
Coconut Beef Curry	102
Classic Sirloin Tips with Gravy	104
Moist & Tender Chuck Roast	106
Honey Pork Roast	108
Simple Meatballs	109
Shredded Thyme Pork	110
Pineapple Cinnamon Pork	112
Superb Banana Dessert	114
Rhubarb Dessert	115
Plum Delight	116
Refreshing Fruits Dish	117
Dessert Stew	118
Original Fruits Dessert	119
Delicious Apples and Cinnamon	120
Crazy Delicious Pudding	121
Wonderful Berry Pudding	123
Winter Fruits Dessert	125
Different Dessert	126
Orange Dessert	127
Great Pumpkin Dessert	129

Delicious Baked Apples 131
Moist Pumpkin Brownie 133
Lemon Custard 135
Pumpkin Pudding 137
Easy Yogurt Custard 139
Zucchini Pudding 141
Delicious Pina Colada 142
Apple Caramel Cake 143
Apple Rice Pudding 144
Vegan Coconut Risotto Pudding 145
Vanilla Avocado Pudding 146
Vanilla Almond Risotto 148
Coconut Raspberry Curd 149
Simple Chocolate Mousse 151
The Best Tropical Dessert Ever 153
Crème with Almond and Chocolate 155
Cinnamon Flan 157
Yummy Upside-Down Cake 159
Extraordinary Chocolate Cheesecake 161
Old-School Cheesecake 163
Sweet and Sour Tale Cake 165
Lazy Sunday Cake 167
Keto Chocolate Brownies 169
Sweet Porridge with a Twist 171

Cheesecake Tropicana 172

Classic Holiday Custard 174

Blackberry Espresso Brownies 176

Sweet Porridge with Blueberries 178

Vanilla Berry Cupcakes 180

Mini Cheesecakes with Berries 182

Special Berry Crisp with Cinnamon 184

Yummy Fire Cheesecake 186

Classic Carrot Cake 188

Classic Brownie with Blackberry-Goat Cheese Swirl 190

Special Birthday Cake 193

Holiday Blueberry Pudding 195

Fluffy Strawberry Cake 197

Chocolate Cheesecake 200

Raspberry Compote 202

Chocolate Cream 204

Butter Pancakes 206

Lemon Cupcakes with Blueberries 208

Chocolate Brownies 210

Peach Pie 212

Almond Butter Cookies 214

Mini Brownie Cakes 216

Hot Chicken Soup

Preparation Time: 20 minutes

Servings 5

Nutritional Values per serving: 238 Calories; 17g Fat; 5.4g Total Carbs; 16.4g Protein; 2.6g Sugars

Ingredients

- 2 tablespoons grapeseed oil
- 2 banana shallots, chopped
- 4 cloves garlic, minced
- 1 cup Cremini mushrooms, sliced
- 2 bell peppers, seeded and sliced
- 1 serrano pepper, seeded and sliced
- 2 ripe tomatoes, pureed
- 1 teaspoon porcini powder
- 2 tablespoons dry white wine
- Sea salt and ground black pepper, to your liking
- 1 teaspoon dried basil
- 1/2 teaspoon dried dill weed
- 5 cups broth, preferably homemade
- 4 chicken wings

Directions

1. Press the "Sauté" button and heat the oil. Once hot, sauté the shallots until just tender and aromatic.

2. Add the garlic, mushrooms, and peppers; cook an additional 3 minutes or until softened.
3. Now, stir in tomatoes, porcini powder, white wine, salt, and black pepper. Add the remaining ingredients and stir to combine.
4. Secure the lid. Choose "Manual" mode and High pressure; cook for 18 minutes. Once cooking is complete, use a quick pressure release.
5. Make sure to release any remaining steam and carefully remove the lid. Remove the chicken wings from the Instant Pot. Discard the bones and chop the meat.
6. Add the chicken meat back to the Instant Pot. Ladle into individual bowls and serve warm. Bon appétit!

Chicken Fillets with Bacon and Cheese

Preparation Time: 25 minutes

Servings 6

Nutritional Values per serving: 450 Calories; 24.1g Fat; 2.5g Total Carbs; 53.6g Protein; 0.2g Sugars

Ingredients

- 1 ¼ cups water
- 10 ounces Ricotta cheese, crumbled
- 6 chicken fillets
- Salt, to taste
- 1/2 teaspoon cayenne pepper
- 6 tablespoons bacon crumbles
- 4 ounces Monterey-Jack cheese
- 1 tablespoon chicken bouillon granules

Directions

1. Add water to the bottom of the Instant Pot. Add Ricotta cheese and chicken fillets; sprinkle with salt and cayenne pepper.
2. Secure the lid. Choose "Manual" mode and High pressure; cook for 18 minutes. Once cooking is complete, use a quick pressure release.
3. Now, shred the chicken with two forks and return it back to the Instant Pot. Stir in bacon crumbles, cheese, and chicken bouillon granules.

4. Place the lid back on the Instant Pot, press the "Sauté" button and cook an additional 4 minutes. Divide among serving plates and serve immediately. Bon appétit!

Mediterranean Chicken Wraps

Preparation Time: 20 minutes

Servings 6

Nutritional Values per serving: 238 Calories; 9.5g Fat; 6.1g Total Carbs; 29.1g Protein; 4.1g Sugars

Ingredients

- 1 ½ pounds chicken tenderloin, cut into 1/2-inch pieces
- Salt and black pepper, to taste
- 1 teaspoon dried oregano
- 1/2 teaspoon dried basil
- 1/2 teaspoon ground cumin
- 1 cup water
- 2 ripe tomatoes, pureed
- 2 garlic cloves, minced
- 1 tablespoon golden Greek peppers, minced
- 1 tablespoon freshly squeezed lemon juice
- 1 large-sized head lettuce
- 6 ounces Feta cheese, cubed
- 1 ounce Kalamata olives, pitted and sliced
- 2 Florina peppers, seeded and chopped

Directions

1. Add the chicken, salt, black pepper, oregano, basil, cumin, and water to your Instar Pot.
2. Secure the lid. Choose the "Manual" setting and High pressure; cook for 10 minutes. Once cooking is complete, use a natural pressure release; carefully remove the lid. Reserve the chicken.
3. Then, add tomatoes, garlic, and Greek peppers to the Instant Pot.
4. Press the "Sauté" button and cook for 6 minutes at Low pressure. Add the shredded chicken back into the Instant Pot.
5. To serve, divide the chicken mixture among lettuce leaves. Top with Feta cheese, olives, and Florina peppers. Roll up in taco-style, serve and enjoy!

Family Chicken Wings

Preparation Time: 45 minutes

Servings 6

Nutritional Values per serving: 301 Calories; 19g Fat; 3.5g Total Carbs; 27.4g Protein; 2.1g Sugars

Ingredients

- 1 ½ pounds chicken wings, bone-in, skin-on
- 1 tablespoon olive oil
- 1 tablespoon balsamic vinegar
- 1 tablespoon Shoyu sauce
- 2 tablespoons ketchup
- 1 cup water
- Sea salt, to taste
- 1/2 teaspoon cayenne pepper
- 1 cup mayonnaise
- 1 tablespoon sweet paprika

Directions

1. Place chicken wings, olive oil, balsamic vinegar, Shoyu sauce, ketchup, water, salt and cayenne pepper, and granulated garlic in a mixing dish.
2. Let it marinate for 30 minutes in the refrigerator. Secure the lid.

3. Now, press the "Manual" button. Cook the chicken wings along with their marinade for 14 minutes under High pressure.
4. Once cooking is complete, use a natural pressure release; carefully remove the lid.
5. In the meantime, mix mayonnaise with sweet paprika until it is well incorporated. Serve chicken wings with the paprika mayo for dipping. Bon appétit!

Chicken Fillets with Cheese Dip

Preparation Time: 15 minutes

Servings 4

Nutritional Values per serving: 314 Calories; 20.3g Fat; 1.7g Total Carbs; 29.9g Protein; 1.5g Sugars

Ingredients

- 1 tablespoon peanut oil
- 1 pound chicken fillets
- Salt and freshly ground black pepper, to taste
- 1/2 teaspoon dried basil
- 1 cup broth, preferably homemade
- Cheese Sauce:
- 3 teaspoons butter, at room temperature
- 1/3 cup double cream
- 1/3 cup Neufchâtel cheese, at room temperature
- 1/3 cup Gruyère cheese, preferably freshly grated
- 3 tablespoons milk
- 1/2 teaspoon granulated garlic
- 1 teaspoon shallot powder

Directions

1. Press the "Sauté" button and add peanut oil. Once hot, sear the chicken fillets for 3 minutes per side.

2. Season the chicken fillets with salt, black pepper, and basil; pour in the broth.
3. Secure the lid. Choose the "Manual" setting and cook for 6 minutes. Once cooking is complete, use a natural pressure release; carefully remove the lid.
4. Clean the Instant Pot and press the "Sauté" button. Now, melt the butter and add double cream, Neufchâtel cheese, Gruyère cheese and milk; add granulated garlic and shallot powder.
5. Cook until everything is heated through. Bon appétit!

Mexican-Style Chicken Tacos

Preparation Time: 30 minutes

Servings 6

Nutritional Values per serving: 443 Calories; 17.3g Fat; 4.6g Total Carbs; 63.7g Protein; 1.7g Sugars

Ingredients

- Low Carb Tortillas:
- 2 ounces pork rinds, crushed into a powder
- A pinch of baking soda
- A pinch of salt
- 2 ounces ricotta cheese
- 3 eggs
- 1/4 cup water
- Nonstick cooking spray
- **Chicken:**
    - 1 ½ pounds chicken legs, skinless
    - 4 cloves garlic, pressed or chopped
    - 1/2 cup scallions, chopped
    - 1 teaspoon dried basil
    - 1/2 teaspoon dried thyme
    - 1/2 teaspoon dried rosemary
    - 1 teaspoon dried oregano
    - Sea salt, to your liking

- 1/3 teaspoon ground black pepper
- 1/4 cup freshly squeezed lemon juice
- 1 cup water
- 1/4 cup dry white wine
- 1/2 cup salsa, preferably homemade

Directions

1. To make low carb tortillas, add pork rinds, baking soda, and salt to your food processor; pulse a few times.
2. Now, fold in the cheese and eggs; mix until well combined. Add the water and process until smooth and uniform.
3. Spritz a pancake pan with a nonstick cooking spray. Preheat the pancake pan over moderate heat.
4. Now, pour the batter into the pan and prepare like you would a tortilla. Reserve keeping the tortillas warm.
5. Then, press the "Sauté" button and cook chicken legs for 2 to 4 minutes per side; reserve. Add the garlic and scallions and cook until aromatic.
6. Add the remaining ingredients, except for salsa. Return the chicken legs back to the Instant Pot.
7. Secure the lid. Choose the "Poultry" setting and cook for 15 minutes. Once cooking is complete, use a quick pressure release; carefully remove the lid.

8. Shred the chicken with two forks and discard the bones; serve with prepared tortillas and salsa. Enjoy!

Southern Chicken Stew

Preparation Time: 25 minutes

Servings 6

Nutritional Values per serving: 453 Calories; 22.6g Fat; 5.9g Total Carbs; 53.6g Protein; 2.6g Sugars

Ingredients

- 2 slices bacon
- 6 chicken legs, skinless and boneless
- 3 cups water
- 2 chicken bouillon cubes
- 1 leek, chopped
- 1 carrot, trimmed and chopped
- 4 garlic cloves, minced
- 1/2 teaspoon dried thyme
- 1/2 teaspoon dried basil
- 1 teaspoon Hungarian paprika
- 1 bay leaf
- 1 cup double cream
- 1/2 teaspoon ground black pepper

Directions

1. Press the "Sauté" button to heat up your Instant Pot. Now, cook the bacon, crumbling it with a spatula; cook until the bacon is crisp and reserve.

2. Now, add the chicken legs and cook until browned on all sides.
3. Add the water, bouillon cubes, leeks, carrot, garlic, thyme, basil, paprika, andbay leaf; stir to combine.
4. Secure the lid. Choose the "Poultry" setting and cook for 15 minutes at High pressure. Once cooking is complete, use a natural pressure release; carefully remove the lid.
5. Fold in the cream and allow it to cook in the residual heat, stirring continuously. Ladle into individual bowls, sprinkle each serving with freshly grated black pepper and serve warm. Bon appétit!

Turkey Chowder with Swiss Chard

Preparation Time: 35 minutes

Servings 6

Nutritional Values per serving: 188 Calories; 9.2g Fat; 6.9g Total Carbs; 17.7g Protein; 3.2g Sugars

Ingredients

- 1 tablespoon canola oil
- 1 pound turkey thighs
- 1 carrot, trimmed and chopped
- 1 leek, chopped
- 1 parsnip, chopped
- 2 garlic cloves, minced
- 1 ½ quarts turkey broth
- 2 star anise pods
- Sea salt, to taste
- 1/4 teaspoon ground black pepper, or more to taste
- 1 bay leaf
- 1 bunch fresh Thai basil
- 1/4 teaspoon dried dill
- 1/2 teaspoon turmeric powder
- 2 cups Swiss chard, torn into pieces

Directions

1. Press the "Sauté" button and heat the canola oil. Now, brown turkey thighs for 2 to 3 minutes on each side; reserve.
2. Add a splash of turkey broth to scrape up any browned bits from the bottom.
3. Then, add the carrot, leek, parsnip and garlic to the Instant Pot. Sauté until they are softened.
4. Add remaining turkey broth, star anise pods, salt, black pepper, bay leaf, Thai basil, dill, and turmeric powder.
5. Secure the lid. Choose the "Soup" setting and cook for 30 minutes. Once cooking is complete, use a natural pressure release; carefully remove the lid.
6. Stir in Swiss chard while still hot to wilt leaves. Enjoy!

Instant Cheesy Chicken Drumsticks

Preparation Time: 25 minutes

Servings 5

Nutritional Values per serving: 409 Calories; 23.8g Fat; 4.8g Total Carbs; 41.7g Protein; 2.4g Sugars

Ingredients

- 1 tablespoon olive oil
- 5 chicken drumsticks
- 1/2 teaspoon marjoram
- 1/2 teaspoon thyme
- 1 teaspoon shallot powder
- 2 garlic cloves, minced
- 1/2 cup chicken stock
- 1/4 cup dry white wine
- 1/4 cup full-fat milk
- 6 ounces ricotta cheese
- 4 ounces cheddar cheese
- 1/4 teaspoon ground black pepper
- 1/2 teaspoon cayenne pepper
- Sea salt, to taste

Directions

1. Press the "Sauté" button and heat the oil. Once hot, brown chicken drumsticks for 3 minutes; turn the chicken over and cook an additional 3 minutes,
2. Now, add marjoram, thyme, shallot powder, garlic, chicken stock, wine, and milk.
3. Secure the lid. Choose the "Manual" setting and cook for 15 minutes. Once cooking is complete, use a natural pressure release; carefully remove the lid.
4. Shred the chicken meat and return to the Instant Pot. Press the "Sauté" button and stir in ricotta cheese, cheddar cheese, black pepper, and cayenne pepper.
5. Cook for a couple of minutes longer or until the cheese melts and everything is heated through.
6. Season with sea salt, taste and adjust the seasonings. Bon appétit!

Spicy Chicken Wingettes

Preparation Time: 1 hour 15 minutes

Servings 6

Nutritional Values per serving: 296 Calories; 22.5g Fat; 6.9g Total Carbs; 10.8g Protein; 3.3g Sugars

Ingredients

- 10 fresh cayenne peppers, trimmed and chopped
- 3 garlic cloves, minced
- 1 ½ cups white vinegar
- 1/2 teaspoon black pepper
- 1 teaspoon sea salt
- 1 teaspoon onion powder
- 12 chicken wingettes
- 2 tablespoons olive oil
- Dipping Sauce:
- 1/2 cup mayonnaise
- 1/2 cup sour cream
- 1/2 cup cilantro, chopped
- 2 cloves garlic, minced
- 1 teaspoon smoked paprika

Directions

1. Place cayenne peppers, 3 garlic cloves, white vinegar, black pepper, salt, and onion powder in a container.

Add chicken wingettes, and let them marinate, covered, for 1 hour in the refrigerator.
2. Add the chicken wingettes, along with the marinade and olive oil to the Instant Pot.
3. Secure the lid. Choose the "Manual" setting and cook for 6 minutes. Once cooking is complete, use a quick pressure release; carefully remove the lid.
4. In a mixing bowl, thoroughly combine mayonnaise, sour cream, cilantro, garlic, and smoked paprika.
5. Serve warm chicken with the dipping sauce on the side. Bon appétit!

Turkey Legs Delight

Preparation Time: 40 minutes

Servings 6

Nutritional Values per serving: 339 Calories; 19.3g Fat; 1.3g Total Carbs; 37.7g Protein; 0.4g Sugars

Ingredients

- 3 tablespoons sesame oil
- 2 pounds turkey legs
- Sea salt and ground black pepper, to your liking
- A bunch of scallions, roughly chopped
- 1 ½ cups turkey broth

Directions

1. Press the "Sauté" button and heat the sesame oil. Now, brown turkey legs on all sides; season with salt and black pepper.
2. Add the scallions and broth.
3. Secure the lid. Choose the "Manual" setting and cook for 35 minutes. Once cooking is complete, use a natural pressure release; carefully remove the lid.
4. You can thicken the cooking liquid on the "Sauté" setting if desired. Serve warm.

Old-Fashioned Paprikash

Preparation Time: 25 minutes

Servings 6

Nutritional Values per serving: 402 Calories; 31.7g Fat; 6.1g Total Carbs; 21g Protein; 3.1g Sugars

Ingredients

- 1 tablespoon lard, at room temperature
- 1 ½ pounds chicken thighs
- 1/2 cup tomato puree
- 1 ½ cups water
- 1 yellow onion, chopped
- 1 large-sized carrot, sliced
- 1 celery stalk, diced
- 2 garlic cloves, minced
- 2 bell peppers, seeded and chopped
- 1 Hungarian wax pepper, seeded and minced
- 1 teaspoon cayenne pepper
- 1 tablespoon Hungarian paprika
- 1 teaspoon coarse salt
- 1/2 teaspoon ground black pepper
- 1/2 teaspoon poultry seasoning
- 6 ounces sour cream
- 1 tablespoon arrowroot powder

- 1 cup water

Directions

1. Press the "Sauté" button to heat up the Instant Pot. Now, melt the lard until hot; sear the chicken thighs for 2 to 3 minutes per side.
2. Add the tomato puree, 1 ½ cups of water, onion, carrot, celery, garlic, peppers, and seasonings.
3. Secure the lid. Choose the "Manual" setting and cook for 20 minutes at High pressure. Once cooking is complete, use a quick pressure release; carefully remove the lid.
4. In the meantime, thoroughly combine sour cream, arrowroot powder and 1 cup of water; whisk to combine well.
5. Add the sour cream mixture to the Instant Pot to thicken the cooking liquid. Cook for a couple of minutes on the residual heat.
6. Ladle into individual bowls and serve immediately.

Medley with Chicken and Mushrooms

Preparation Time: 20 minutes

Servings 8

Nutritional Values per serving: 222 Calories; 12g Fat; 2.5g Total Carbs; 24.6g Protein; 1g Sugars

Ingredients

- 2 teaspoons olive oil
- 2 pounds chicken breast halves, cubed
- 1 teaspoon cayenne pepper
- 1 teaspoon onion powder
- 1/2 teaspoon porcini powder
- Sea salt, to taste
- 1/4 teaspoon freshly ground black pepper, or more to taste
- 1 cup white mushrooms, thinly sliced
- 1 parsnip, chopped
- 4 garlic cloves, minced
- 2 cups vegetable broth
- 2 bay leaves
- 1/2 cup half-and-half cream
- 2 heaping tablespoons fresh cilantro

Directions

1. Press the "Sauté" button to heat up the Instant Pot. Now, heat the oil until sizzling. Then, cook the chicken breast for 4 to 6 minutes, turning them over a few times.
2. Add cayenne pepper, onion powder, porcini powder, salt, black pepper, and white mushrooms. Continue to sauté until they are fragrant.
3. Now, stir in parsnip, garlic, broth, and bay leaves.
4. Secure the lid. Choose the "Manual" setting and cook for 10 minutes at High pressure. Once cooking is complete, use a quick pressure release; carefully remove the lid.
5. Add half-and-half cream and stir until the cooking liquid is slightly thickened. Serve garnished with fresh cilantro. Bon appétit!

Instant Chicken Teriyaki

Preparation Time: 15 minutes

Servings 6

Nutritional Values per serving: 326 Calories; 13.2g Fat; 3.1g Total Carbs; 45.6g Protein; 0.7g Sugars

Ingredients

- 1/3 cup coconut aminos
- 1/4 cup rice wine vinegar
- 3 tablespoons Mirin
- 8 drops liquid stevia
- 1 tablespoon cornstarch
- 1/3 cup water
- 2 tablespoons olive oil
- 2 pounds chicken legs, boneless and skinless
- 1 teaspoon garlic powder
- 1 teaspoon ginger powder
- Sea salt and black pepper, to taste
- 1/2 teaspoon sweet paprika
- 2/3 cup chicken stock

Directions

1. Press the "Sauté" button to heat up your Instant Pot. Now, add the coconut aminos, vinegar, Mirin, liquid stevia, and cornstarch; whisk to combine well.

2. Now, pour in water and cook, bringing to a boil; cook until the liquid is thickened; reserve teriyaki sauce.
3. Wipe down the Instant Pot with a damp cloth; then, heat olive oil and cook the chicken until browned. Add garlic powder andginger powder.
4. Season with salt, black pepper, and paprika.
5. Add chicken stockand 2/3 of teriyaki sauce; stir to combine. Secure the lid. Choose the "Manual" setting and cook for 10 minutes.
6. Once cooking is complete, use a natural pressure release; carefully remove the lid. Serve with the remaining 1/3 of teriyaki sauce and enjoy!

Lazy Chicken Carnitas

Preparation Time: 20 minutes

Servings 8

Nutritional Values per serving: 294 Calories; 15.4g Fat; 2.8g Total Carbs; 35.2g Protein; 1.3g Sugars

Ingredients

- 3 pounds whole chicken, cut into pieces
- 3 cloves garlic, pressed
- 1 guajillo chili, minced
- 1 tablespoon avocado oil
- 1/3 cup roasted vegetable broth
- Sea salt, to taste
- 1/2 teaspoon ground bay leaf
- 1/3 teaspoon cayenne pepper
- 1/2 teaspoon paprika
- 1/3 teaspoon black pepper
- 1 cup crème fraiche, to serve
- 2 heaping tablespoons fresh coriander, chopped

Directions

1. Place all of the above ingredients, except for crème fraiche and fresh coriander, in the Instant Pot.

2. Secure the lid. Choose the "Poultry" setting and cook for 15 minutes. Once cooking is complete, use a quick pressure release; carefully remove the lid.
3. Shred the chicken with two forks and discard the bones. Add a dollop of crème fraiche to each serving and garnish with fresh coriander. Enjoy!

Tasty Chicken Goulash

Preparation Time: 25 minutes

Servings 6

Nutritional Values per serving: 353 Calories; 19.5g Fat; 6.5g Total Carbs; 34.3g Protein; 4.3g Sugars

Ingredients

- 1 tablespoon olive oil
- 2 pounds chicken breast halves, boneless and skinless
- 2 small-sized shallots, chopped
- 1 teaspoon garlic paste
- 1 cup milk
- 2 ripe tomatoes, chopped
- 1 teaspoon curry powder
- 1 tablespoon tamari sauce
- 1 tablespoon balsamic vinegar
- 2 tablespoons vermouth
- Sea salt, to taste
- 1/2 teaspoon cayenne pepper
- 1/3 teaspoon black pepper
- 1/2 teaspoon hot paprika
- 1/2 teaspoon ginger, freshly grated
- 1 celery stalk with leaves, chopped
- 1 bell pepper, chopped

- 1 tablespoon flaxseed meal

Directions

1. Press the "Sauté" button to heat up the Instant Pot. Now, add olive oil. Once hot, sear the chicken breast halves for 3 to 4 minutes per side.
2. Add the shallots, garlic, milk, tomatoes, curry powder, tamari sauce, vinegar, vermouth, salt, cayenne pepper, black pepper, hot paprika, ginger, celery and bell pepper to the Instant Pot; stir to combine well.
3. Secure the lid. Choose the "Meat/Stew" setting and cook for 20 minutes at High pressure. Once cooking is complete, use a quick pressure release; carefully remove the lid.
4. Add flaxseed meal and continue stirring in the residual heat. Ladle into serving bowls and enjoy!

Turkey Meatloaf with Parmigiano-Reggiano

Preparation Time: 35 minutes

Servings 6

Nutritional Values per serving: 449 Calories; 29.7g Fat; 6.1g Total Carbs; 36.2g Protein; 3.2g Sugars

Ingredients

- 2 pounds ground turkey
- 2/3 cup pork rind crumbs
- 1/2 cup Parmigiano-Reggiano, grated
- 1 tablespoon coconut aminos
- 2 eggs, chopped
- Sea salt, to taste
- 1/4 teaspoon ground black pepper
- 1 yellow onion, peeled and chopped
- 2 garlic cloves, minced
- 4 ounces tomato paste
- 1 tablespoon Italian seasoning
- 1/2 cup tomato sauce
- 1 cup water
- 1 teaspoon mustard powder
- 1/2 teaspoon chili powder

Directions

1. Prepare your Instant Pot by adding a metal rack and 1 ½ cups of water to the bottom of the inner pot.
2. In a large mixing bowl, thoroughly combine ground turkey with pork rind crumbs, Parmigiano-Reggiano, coconut aminos, eggs, salt, black pepper, onion, garlic, tomato paste, Italian seasoning.
3. Shape this mixture into a meatloaf; lower your meatloaf onto the metal rack.
4. Then, in a mixing bowl, thoroughly combine tomato sauce with water, mustard and chili powder. Spread this mixture over the top of your meatloaf.
5. Secure the lid. Choose the "Meat/Stew" setting and cook for 20 minutes at High pressure. Once cooking is complete, use a natural pressure release; carefully remove the lid.
6. Afterwards, place your meatloaf under the preheated broiler for 5 minutes. Allow the meatloaf to rest for 6 to 8 minutes before slicing and serving. Bon appétit!

Southern Turkey Soup

Preparation Time: 20 minutes

Servings 4

Nutritional Values per serving: 429 Calories; 26.2g Fat; 6.7g Total Carbs; 40.2g Protein; 3.1g Sugars

Ingredients

- 2 teaspoons coconut oil
- 2 onions, chopped
- 2 garlic cloves, finely chopped
- 1/2 teaspoon freshly grated ginger
- 2 tomatoes, chopped
- 1 celery stalk with leaves, chopped
- 1 teaspoon dried basil
- 1/2 teaspoon dried rosemary
- 1 bay leaf
- 1/4 teaspoon freshly ground black pepper
- 1/2 teaspoon red pepper flakes, crushed
- Sea salt, to taste
- 3 turkey thighs
- 4 cups roasted vegetable broth
- 1/4 cup fresh parsley, finely minced

Directions

1. Press the "Sauté" button to heat up the Instant Pot. Now, heat the oil. Cook the onion and garlic until softened and aromatic.
2. Add grated ginger, tomatoes, celery, basil, rosemary, bay leaf, black pepper, red pepper, salt, turkey thighs and vegetable broth.
3. Secure the lid. Choose the "Manual" setting and cook for 15 minutes at High pressure. Once cooking is complete, use a quick pressure release; carefully remove the lid.
4. Remove turkey thighs from the soup; discard the bones, shred the meat and return it to the Instant Pot.
5. Add fresh parsley and stir well. Serve in individual bowls. Bon appétit!

Thai-Style Chicken

Preparation Time: 15 minutes

Servings 4

Nutritional Values per serving: 192 Calories; 7.5g Fat; 5.4g Total Carbs; 25.2g Protein; 2.2g Sugars

Ingredients

- 1 tablespoon coconut oil
- 1 pound chicken, cubed
- 1 shallot, peeled and chopped
- 2 cloves garlic, minced
- 1 teaspoon fresh ginger root, julienned
- 1/3 teaspoon cumin powder
- 1 teaspoon Thai chili, minced
- 1 cup vegetable broth, preferably homemade
- 1 tomato, peeled and chopped
- 1/3 cup coconut milk, unsweetened
- 1 teaspoon Thai curry paste
- 2 tablespoons tamari sauce
- 1/2 cup sprouts
- Salt and freshly ground black pepper, to taste

Directions

1. Press the "Sauté" button to heat up the Instant Pot. Now, heat the coconut oil. Cook the chicken for 2 to 3 minutes, stirring frequently; reserve.
2. Then, in pan drippings, cook the shallot and garlic until softened; add a splash of vegetable broth, if needed.
3. Add ginger, cumin powder and Thai chili and cook until aromatic or 1 minute more.
4. Now, stir in vegetable broth, tomato, coconut milk, Thai curry paste, and tamari sauce.
5. Secure the lid. Choose the "Manual" setting and cook for 10 minutes under High pressure. Once cooking is complete, use a quick pressure release; carefully remove the lid.
6. Afterwards, add sprouts, salt, and black pepper and serve immediately. Bon appétit!

Chicken Thighs with Green Beans and Potatoes

Prep Time: 8 Mins

Total Time: 25 Mins

Serving: 6

Ingredients:

- 2 pounds Chicken Thighs
- 1 pound Green Beans
- 1 pound Potatoes, peeled and halved
- Juice of 1 Lemon
- 2 tbsp Olive Oil
- 1 tbsp Ghee
- ½ cup Chicken Stock
- 1 tsp mixed Herbs
- 1 tsp minced Garlic

Direction

1. Set your Instant Pot to SAUTE and melt the ghee along with the olive oil in it.
2. Add garlic and cook for 1 minute.
3. Add the chicken thighs and cook them on all sides, until they become golden.
4. Stir in the lemon juice and herbs and cook for an additional minute.

5. Add the remaining ingredients and stir well to combine.
6. Close the lid and set the IP to MANUAL.
7. Cook for 15 minutes on HIGH.
8. Release the pressure quickly.
9. Serve and enjoy!

Nutritional Values per serving:

Calories 500

Total Fats 27g

Carbs: 19g

Protein 45g

Dietary Fiber: 3g

Quick and Easy Garlic Shredded Chicken

Prep Time: 5 Mins

Total Time: 25 Mins

Serving: 4

Ingredients:

- 1 tsp Garlic Powder
- 1 ¾ pounds Chicken Breasts
- ¼ tsp Black Pepper
- 1 cup Homemade Chicken Broth

Direction

1. Simply dump all of the ingredients in the Instant Pot.
2. Give the mixture a good stir and put the lid on.
3. Turn it clockwise to seal.
4. Set the IP to MANUAL.
5. Cook on HIGH for 20 minutes.
6. Do a quick pressure release and open the lid.
7. Shred the chicken inside the pot with 2 forks.
8. Serve and enjoy!

Nutritional Values per serving:

Calories 430

Total Fats 17g

Carbs: 0g

Protein 45g

Dietary Fiber: 0g

The Ultimate Mexican Chicken

Prep Time: 5 Mins

Total Time: 25 Mins

Serving: 6

Ingredients:

- 2 pounds Chicken Breasts
- Juice of 1 Lime
- 1 Jalapeno, seeded and diced
- ½ tsp Chili Powder
- ½ tsp Cumin
- 1 Green Bell Pepper, diced
- 1 Red Bell Pepper, diced
- 10 ounces Tomatoes, diced
- 1 Red Onion, diced
- 1 tbsp Olive Oil
- Pinch of Black Pepper

Direction

1. Set the IP to SAUTE and add the olive oil.
2. When sizzling, add the onion and peppers and cook for 3-4 minutes, until soft.
3. Add the rest of the ingredients.
4. Stir to combine and close the lid.
5. Set the Instant Pot to MANUAL.

6. Cook the chicken for 15 minutes on HIGH pressure.
7. Do a quick pressure release and open the lid.
8. Shred the chicken with two forks and stir to combine. This step is optional, you can serve the chicken as it is and garnish with the cooking liquid and veggies on top.
9. Enjoy!

Nutritional Values per serving:

Calories 340

Total Fats 14g

Carbs: 10g

Protein 45g

Dietary Fiber: 2g

Instant Rotisserie Chicken

Prep Time: 5 Mins

Total Time: 40 Mins

Serving: 4

Ingredients:

- 1 Whole Chicken About 2 ½ - 3 lb
- 1 ½ tbsp Olive Oil
- 1 cup Homemade Chicken Broth
- 1 tsp Smoked Paprika
- 1 tsp Garlic Powder

Direction

1. Wash the chicken well and pat dry with some paper towels.
2. In a small bowl, combine the paprika, garlic powder, and oil.
3. Rub this mixture into the chicken.
4. Set your Instant Pot to SAUTE and place the chicken inside.
5. Sear on all sides, until it turns golden.
6. Pour the broth around the chicken and close the lid.
7. Set the IP to MANUAL and cook on HIGH for 25 minutes.
8. Release the pressure quickly.

9. Let sit for 10 minutes before serving.
10. Enjoy!

Nutritional Values per serving:

Calories 585

Total Fats 20g

Carbs: 0.7g

Protein 95g

Dietary Fiber: 0.3g

Turkey with Leeks and Mushrooms

Prep Time: 8 Mins

Total Time: 25 Mins

Serving: 6

Ingredients:

- 2 pounds Turkey Breasts, cut into large pieces
- 2 tbsp Arrowroot
- ½ cup Homemade Chicken Broth
- ½ cup Almond Milk
- 2 Leeks, sliced
- 4 tbsp Ghee
- 1 ¼ pounds Mushrooms, sliced
- ¼ tsp Garlic Powder
- ¼ tsp Black Pepper

Direction

1. Season the turkey with garlic powder and pepper.
2. Set your IP to SAUTE and add the ghee.
3. When melted, add the turkey pieces and cook until they are no longer pink. Transfer them to a plate.
4. Add the leeks and mushrooms to the IP and cook for 3 minutes.
5. Return the turkey to the pot and pour the broth over.
6. Close the lid and cook for 8 minutes on HIGH.

7. Release the pressure naturally.
8. Whisk together the almond milk and arrowroot and stir into the pot.
9. Cook on SAUTE until thickened.
10. Serve and enjoy!

Nutritional Values per serving:

Calories 555

Total Fats 24g

Carbs: 37g

Protein 50g

Dietary Fiber: 3g

Chicken with Onion and Green Olives

Prep Time: 5 Mins

Total Time: 20 Mins

Serving: 4

Ingredients:

- 4 Chicken Breasts
- 1 can Green Olives, pitted
- ½ cup Red Onion, sliced
- 1 cup Homemade Chicken Broth
- 2 tbsp Ghee
- 2 tbsp Lemon Juice
- Pinch of Pepper

Direction

1. Set your Instant Pot to SAUTE and add the ghee.
2. When melted, add the chicken and brown on all sides.
3. Add the rest of the ingredients and put the lid on.
4. Set the Instant Pot to MANUAL and cook on HIGH for 10 minutes.
5. Do a quick pressure release.
6. Serve and enjoy!

Nutritional Values per serving:

Calories 500

Total Fats 34g

Carbs: 2g

Protein 44g

Dietary Fiber: 0.5g

Juicy and Fall-off-Bone Drumsticks

Prep Time: 5 Mins

Total Time: 45 Mins

Serving: 3

Ingredients:

- 6 Chicken Drumsticks
- ½ Bell Pepper, diced
- 2 tsp minced Garlic
- 1 tbsp Olive Oil
- 2 cups Water
- ½ Red Onion, diced
- 2 tbsp Tomato Paste
- Pinch of Pepper

Direction

1. Set your IP to SAUTE and heat the olive oil in it.
2. Add the onions and pepper and cook for 3 minutes.
3. Add the garlic and cook for an additional minute.
4. Place the drumsticks inside.
5. Whisk together the tomato paste and water and pour the mixture over the drumsticks.
6. Put the lid on and seal.
7. Set the IP to MANUAL.
8. Cook on HIGH for 15 minutes.

9. Let the pressure drop on its own.
10. Serve and enjoy!

Nutritional Values per serving:

Calories 450

Total Fats 27g

Carbs: 5.3g

Protein 42g

Dietary Fiber: 1.4g

Slow-Cooked Turkey

Prep Time: 15 Mins

Total Time: 4 hours and 15 Mins

Serving: 4

Ingredients:

- 1 ½ pounds Turkey Breasts
- 1 tbsp Organic Dijon Mustard
- 2 tbsp Olive Oil
- 2 tsp Smoked Paprika
- 1 tsp minced Garlic
- Pinch of Black Pepper
- 1 cup Homemade Chicken Broth

Direction

1. Set your Instant Pot to SAUTE and add the oil to it.
2. When hot and sizzling, add the turkey and cook until it becomes brown.
3. Whisk together ½ of the broth and the rest of the ingredients and pour over the turkey.
4. Close the lid and set the IP to SLOW COOK.
5. Cook for 2 hours.
6. Do a quick pressure release and pour the remaining broth over.
7. Seal the lid again and cook for another 2 hours.

8. Do a quick pressure release.
9. Serve and enjoy!

Nutritional Values per serving:

Calories 400

Total Fats 30g

Carbs: 2.5g

Protein 40g

Dietary Fiber: 0.5g

Mediterranean Chicken Wings

Prep Time: 15 Mins

Total Time: 10 Mins

Serving: 4

Ingredients:

- 12 Chicken Wings
- 2 tsp Tarragon
- 1 tbsp Oregano
- 6 tbsp Homemade Chicken Broth
- ¼ cup Homemade Chicken Broth
- 2 tbsp Olive Oil
- 1 tbsp Garlic Puree
- 1 tbsp Basil
- Pinch Pepper
- 1 cup of Water

Direction

1. Pour the water into the Instant Pot and lower the rack.
2. In a bowl, combine the remaining ingredients.
3. Let sit for 15 minutes.
4. Transfer the chicken wings to a baking dish.
5. Place the dish on the rack and close the lid of the IP.
6. Set the Instant Pot to MANUAL and cook for 10 minutes on HIGH.

7. Do a quick pressure release.
8. Serve and enjoy!

Nutritional Values per serving:

Calories 160

Total Fats 13g

Carbs: 0.6g

Protein 11g

Dietary Fiber: 0g

Green Chicken

Prep Time: 8 Mins

Total Time: 20 Mins

Serving: 4

Ingredients:

- 1 1/3 pounds Chicken Breasts, cubed
- 1 cup chopped Spinach
- 1/3 cup Basil Leaves
- 1/3 cup Coconut Cream
- 2/3 cup Homemade Chicken Broth
- 1 tsp minced Garlic
- 1 tbsp Olive Oil

Direction

1. Heat the oil in the Instant Pot on SAUTE.
2. Add the garlic and cook for 1 minute.
3. Add the chicken and cook until it is no longer pink.
4. Stir in the rest of the ingredients.
5. Put the lid on and seal.
6. Set the IP to MANUAL.
7. Cook on HIGH for 8 minutes.
8. Do a quick pressure release.
9. Serve and enjoy!

Nutritional Values per serving:

Calories 320

Total Fats 14g

Carbs: 4g

Protein 35g

Dietary Fiber: 1g

Juicy Herbed Turkey Breasts

Prep Time: 10 Mins

Total Time: 20 Mins

Serving: 3

Ingredients:

- 1 pound Turkey Breasts
- ¼ tsp Oregano
- ¼ tsp Thyme
- 2 tbsp chopped Basil
- 1 tbsp chopped Parsley
- Pinch of Pepper
- ¼ tsp Garlic Powder
- 1 tbsp Olive Oil
- 1 cup Water

Direction

1. Heat the oil in the IP on SAUTE.
2. Add the turkey and cook until it becomes browned on all sides.
3. Stir in the herbs and spices and pour the water over.
4. Close the lid and set the Instant Pot to MANUAL.
5. Cook on HIGH for 10 minutes.
6. Do a quick pressure release.
7. Serve as desired and enjoy!

Nutritional Values per serving:

Calories 320

Total Fats 15g

Carbs: 0g

Protein 40g

Dietary Fiber: 0g

Chicken Spaghetti Squash with Shitakes

Prep Time: 8 Mins

Total Time: 40 Mins

Serving: 6

Ingredients:

- 1 cup sliced Shitake Mushrooms
- 2 pounds Chicken Breasts, chopped
- 1 Spaghetti Squash
- 1 cup Homemade Chicken Broth
- 1 tbsp Arrowroot
- 1 cup Water
- 1 tbsp Coconut Oil

Direction

1. Pour the water into the IP.
2. Place the spaghetti squash inside the steamer basket and lower it into the IP.
3. Close the lid and set the IP to MANUAL.
4. Cook for 20 minutes on HIGH.
5. Do a quick pressure release and set aside to cool.
6. Discard the cooking liquid and wipe the IP clean.
7. Set the IP to SAUTE and melt the coconut oil inside.
8. Add the chicken and cook until it becomes golden.
9. Add the rest of the ingredients and close the lid.

10. Cook on HIGH for 8 minutes.
11. Meanwhile, scrape out the flesh of the squash with a fork, into spaghetti-like strings.
12. Do a quick pressure release and open the lid.
13. Stir in the spaghetti.
14. Serve and enjoy!

Nutritional Values per serving:

Calories 260

Total Fats 12g

Carbs: 4g

Protein 22g

Dietary Fiber: 0g

Thai Peanut Chicken

Prep Time: 5 Mins

TotalTime: 33 Mins

Serving: 6

Ingredients:

- 1 ½ cups toasted peanuts
- 1 ½ lb. chicken breasts
- 2 cloves of garlic, minced
- Salt and pepper to taste
- 2 tbsp. chopped scallions for garnish

Directions

1. Place 1 cup of toasted peanuts in a food processor and pulse until smooth. This will serve as your peanut butter. For the remaining half cup of peanut, chop until fine. Set aside.
2. Press the Sauté button on the Instant Pot and place the chicken breasts and garlic. Keep on stirring for 3 minutes until the meat has turned lightly golden.
3. Season with salt and pepper to taste.
4. Pour the peanut butter that you have prepared earlier. Give a good stir and pour a cup of water.
5. Close the lid and seal off the vent.

6. Press the Manual button and adjust the cooking time to 25 minutes.
7. Do natural pressure release.
8. Garnish with chopped nuts and scallions before serving.

Calories:575; Total Fat: 34.8g; Carbs: 2.5g; Dietary Fiber: 0.2g; Protein:42g

Thai Goose with Basil

Prep Time: 10 Mins

Total Time: 40 Mins

Serving: 4

Ingredients:

- 2 tbsp minced Chilies
- 2 tbsp Coconut Oil
- 2 tsp minced Garlic
- 1 tsp minced Ginger
- 2 cups Goose Cubes
- ¼ cup chopped Basil
- 2 tbsp Coconut Aminos
- 1 ½ cups Water

Direction

1. Set your Instant Pot to SAUTE and add half of the coconut oil to it.
2. When melted, add the goose and cook until it becomes browned.
3. Transfer the goose to a baking dish.
4. Add the rest of the ingredients, except the water, to the dish and stir to combine.
5. Pour the water into the IP and lower the trivet.
6. Place the baking dish on the trivet and close the lid.

7. Cook on MANUAL for 10 minutes.
8. Do a quick pressure release.
9. Serve and enjoy!

Nutritional Values per serving:

Calories 190

Total Fats 9g

Carbs: 2g

Protein 27g

Dietary Fiber: 1g

Coconut Kale Chicken

Prep Time: 3 Mins

Total Time: 30 Mins

Serving: 4

Ingredients:

- 1 ½ pounds Chicken Breasts, chopped
- ½ cup canned diced Tomatoes
- ¾ cup Coconut Milk
- 1 cup chopped Kale
- 1 Garlic Clove, minced
- ¼ tsp Onion Powder
- ¼ tsp Paprika
- Pinch of Pepper
- 2/3 cup Homemade Chicken Stock
- ½ tsp Oregano
- 1 tbsp Olive Oil

Direction

1. Heat the oil in the Instant Pot on SAUTE.
2. Add the garlic and cook for 30 seconds.
3. Add chicken, oregano, and spices, and cook until the chicken becomes golden.
4. Pour the stock over and close the lid.
5. Cook on HIGH for 24 minutes.

6. Do a quick pressure release.
7. Open the lid and add the remaining ingredients.
8. Stir to combine and close the lid again.
9. Cook on HIGH for another 4 minutes.
10. Release the pressure quickly and serve drizzled with the sauce.
11. Enjoy!

Nutritional Values per serving:

Calories 455

Total Fats 26g

Carbs: 3g

Protein 55g

Dietary Fiber: 2g

Instant Pot Garlic Chicken

Prep Time: 8 Mins

TotalTime: 40 Mins

Serving: 4

Ingredients:

- 3 tbsp. coconut oil
- 5 cloves of garlic, minced
- 4 chicken breasts, halved
- Salt and pepper to taste
- 1 ½ cups water

Directions

1. Press the Sauté button on the Instant Pot and heat the coconut oil. Sauté the garlic until fragrant then stir in the chicken breasts. Season with salt and pepper to taste.
2. Stir for 5 minutes then pour in water.
3. Close the lid and seal off the vent. Press the Manual button and adjust the cooking time to 30 minutes.
4. Do natural pressure release.

Calories:591; Total Fat: 37.5g; Carbs: 1.1g; Dietary Fiber: 0.7g; Protein: 60.8g

Instant Pot Lemon Olive Chicken

Prep Time: 10 Mins

Total Time: 30 Mins

Serving: 4

Ingredients:

- 4 boneless skinless chicken breasts
- ½ cup coconut oil
- 1/4 teaspoon black pepper
- 1/2 teaspoon cumin
- 1 teaspoon sea salt
- 1 cup Homemade chicken bone-broth
- 2 tbsp. fresh lemon juice
- 1/2 cup red onion, sliced
- 1 can pitted green olives
- 1/2 lemon, thinly sliced

Direction

1. Generously season chicken breasts with cumin, pepper and salt; set your instant pot on sauté mode and melt coconut oil; add chicken and brown both sides.
2. Stir in the remaining ingredients; bring to a gentle simmer and then lock lid.
3. Cook on high for 10 minutes and then use quick release method to release pressure.

4. Serve and enjoy!

Nutritional Values per serving:

Calories 420

Total Fats 38.7g

Carbs: 0.6 g

Protein 42.4g

Dietary Fiber: 0.2g

Instant Pot Chicken Shawarma

Prep Time: 10 Mins

Total Time: 25 Mins

Serving: 8

Ingredients:

- 1 pound chicken thighs
- 1 pound chicken breasts, sliced
- 1/8 teaspoon cinnamon
- 1/4 teaspoon chili powder
- 1 teaspoon ground cumin
- 1/4 teaspoon ground allspice
- 1/4 teaspoon granulated garlic
- 1/2 teaspoon turmeric
- 1 teaspoon paprika
- Pinch of salt
- Pinch of pepper
- 1 cup Homemade chicken broth

Direction

1. Mix all ingredients in your instant pot and lock lid;
2. Cook on poultry setting for 15 minutes and the release pressure naturally.
3. Serve chicken with sauce over mashed sweet potato drizzled with tahini sauce.

Nutritional Values per serving:

Calories 223

Total Fats 8.7g

Carbs: 0.7 g

Protein 35.5g

Dietary Fiber: 0.2g

Italian-Inspired Creamy Chicken

Prep Time: 5 Mins

Cook Time: 15 Mins

Servings: 4

Ingredients:

- 4 boneless, skinless chicken thighs
- 1 teaspoon olive oil
- 1 cup homemade low-sodium chicken broth
- ⅓ cup unsweetened coconut cream or unsweetened almond cream
- 1½ Tablespoons arrowroot powder
- 1 Tablespoon organic basil pesto
- 1 Tablespoon organic Italian seasoning
- 2 Tablespoons organic minced garlic
- 1 Tablespoon organic minced onion
- Pinch of salt, pepper
- Fresh parsley

Direction

1. Press "Sauté" function on Instant Pot. Add olive oil.
2. Once hot, add onion, garlic. Cook 2 minutes. Add chicken. Cook 2 minutes per side, until golden brown. Season with salt, pepper, Italian seasoning. Stir in broth.

3. Lock, seal the lid. Press "Manual" button. Cook on HIGH 8 minutes.
4. When done, naturally release pressure 5 minutes, then quick release. Remove lid.
5. Press "Sauté" function. Stir in arrowroot powder. Stir to coat ingredients. Whisk in coconut cream, basil pesto. Stir. Allow to simmer until thickens. Season if needed.
6. Serve in bowls. Garnish with fresh parsley.

Calories: 242, Fat: 15g, Carbohydrates: 5.3g, Dietary Fiber: 1.8gg, Protein: 26g

Instant Pot Pesto Chicken

Prep Time: 10 Mins

TotalTime: 40 Mins

Serving: 4

Ingredients:

- 2 cups basil leaves
- ¼ cup extra virgin olive oil
- 5 sun-dried tomatoes
- Salt and pepper to taste
- 4 chicken breasts

Directions

1. Put in the food processor the basil leaves, olive oil, and tomatoes. Season with salt and people to taste. Add a cup of water if needed.
2. Place the chicken in the Instant Pot. Pour over the pesto sauce.
3. Close the lid and seal off the vent. Press the Manual button and adjust the cooking time to 30 minutes.

Do natural pressure release.

Calories:556; Total Fat: 32.7g; Carbs: 1.1g; Dietary Fiber: 0.7g; Protein:60.8g

Lemon Chicken

Prep Time: 4 Mins

Cook Time: 15 Mins

Servings: 3

Ingredients:

- 3 boneless, skinless chicken thighs or chicken breasts
- 1/2 small yellow onion, finely chopped
- 2 garlic cloves, minced
- 1 Tablespoons organic Italian seasoning
- 1/4 teaspoon organic smoked or regular paprika
- Zest and juice from 1 lemon
- 1/4 lemon, thinly sliced
- ½ cup homemade low-sodium chicken broth
- 1/4 Tablespoon fresh parsley, finely chopped
- 1 Tablespoons olive oil
- 1/2 Tablespoons ghee clarified butter
- 1/2 teaspoon organic garlic powder
- Pinch of salt, pepper

Direction

1. In a bowl, combine salt, pepper, garlic powder, paprika, Italian seasoning. Coat chicken on all sides with mixture.
2. Press "Sauté" function on Instant Pot. Add the olive oil.

3. Once hot, cook garlic, onions 2 minutes, stirring occasionally. Add chicken. Sear on all sides. Stir in ghee, lemon juice, lemon zest.
4. Place lemon slices on top of chicken.
5. Lock, seal lid. Press "Manual" button. Cook on HIGH 8 minutes.
6. When done, naturally release pressure 5 minutes, then quick release. Remove lid.
7. Serve on a platter. Garnish with fresh parsley, fresh lemon slices. Serve.

Calories: 380, Fat: 22.1g, Carbohydrates: 1.8g, Dietary Fiber: 0.5g, Protein: 42.5g

Delicious Beef Stew

Servings: 4

Cooking Time: 30 minutes

Ingredients:

- 2 ½ lbs chuck roast, boneless
- 1 cup chicken stock
- ½ cup balsamic vinegar
- 1 tbsp Worcestershire sauce
- 1 tbsp soy sauce
- 1 tbsp honey
- ½ tsp red pepper flakes
- 4 garlic cloves, chopped

Directions:

1. Add all ingredients into the instant pot and stir well.
2. Seal pot with lid and cook on high for 30 minutes.
3. Allow to release pressure naturally then open the lid.
4. Serve and enjoy.

Nutritional Values per serving:

Calories: 648; Carbohydrates: 7g; Protein: 94.3g; Fat: 23.7g; Sugar: 5.5g; Sodium: 647mg

Classic Lamb Leg

Servings: 4

Cooking Time: 15 minutes

Ingredients:

- 2 lbs leg of lamb, boneless and cut into chunks
- 2 tbsp tomato paste
- ½ cup beef stock
- 1 tsp oregano, chopped
- 2 tsp thyme, chopped
- 1 tsp rosemary, chopped
- 2 carrots, chopped
- 1 cup onion, chopped
- 1 cup red wine
- 4 garlic cloves, sliced
- 1 tbsp olive oil
- Pepper
- Salt

Directions:

1. Season meat with pepper and salt.
2. Add oil into the instant pot and set the pot on sauté mode.
3. Add meat to the pot and sauté until brown.
4. Add garlic and sauté for 30 seconds.

5. Add red wine and stir well.
6. Add remaining ingredients to the pot and stir well.
7. Seal pot with lid and cook on high for 15 minutes.
8. Allow to release pressure naturally then open the lid.
9. Serve and enjoy.

Nutritional Values per serving:

Calories: 542; Carbohydrates: 10.6g; Protein: 65.3g; Fat: 20.4g; Sugar: 4.2g; Sodium: 343mg

Asian Pork

Servings: 4

Cooking Time: 8 minutes

Ingredients:

- 1 ½ lbs pork shoulder, boneless and cut into strips
- 1 cup scallions, chopped
- 1 tbsp cornstarch
- 1 tbsp water
- 3 cups cabbage, sliced
- 2 garlic cloves, minced
- 1 tbsp sesame oil
- ¼ cup dry sherry
- ¼ cup soy sauce
- ½ cup chicken stock
- 0.5 oz dried mushrooms, cut into pieces

Directions:

1. Add meat into the instant pot along with garlic, oil, sherry, soy sauce, mushrooms, and stock. Stir well.
2. Seal pot with lid and cook on high for 8 minutes.
3. Allow to release pressure naturally then open the lid.
4. Add cabbage and stir well. Cook on sauté mode until cabbage is softened.

5. In a small bowl, mix together cornstarch and 1 tablespoon of water and pour into the pot. Stir until thickened, about 1-2 minutes.
6. Add scallions and stir well.
7. Serve and enjoy.

Nutritional Values per serving:

Calories: 568; Carbohydrates: 8.6g; Protein: 42g; Fat: 40g; Sugar: 2.7g; Sodium: 1124mg

Salsa Pork

Servings: 4

Cooking Time: 15 minutes

Ingredients:

- 2 lbs pork shoulder, boneless and cut into chunks
- ¼ cup fresh cilantro, chopped
- ½ cup chicken stock
- 1 tsp dried oregano
- 1 tsp ground cumin
- 1 tbsp honey
- oz can tomatoes, drained and diced
- 16 oz salsa
- Pepper
- Salt

Directions:
1. Season meat with pepper and salt.
2. Add meat, stock, oregano, cumin, honey, tomatoes, and salsa to the pot.
3. Seal pot with lid and cook on high for 15 minutes.
4. Allow to release pressure naturally then open the lid.
5. Shred the meat using a fork.
6. Add cilantro and stir well.
7. Serve and enjoy.

Nutritional Values per serving:
Calories: 735; Carbohydrates: 17.3g; Protein: 55.7g; Fat: 48.9g; Sugar: 11.4g; Sodium: 1189mg

BBQ Pork Ribs

Servings: 6

Cooking Time: 30 minutes

Ingredients:

- 1 cup water
- 3 lbs pork ribs
- ¼ cup tomato sauce
- 1 cup BBQ sauce
- ½ tsp black pepper
- ½ tsp dried oregano
- 1 tsp garlic powder
- 2 tsp paprika
- 1 tbsp brown sugar
- ½ tsp salt

Directions:

1. In a small bowl, mix together all spices.
2. In another bowl, mix together tomato sauce and ½ cup BBQ sauce.
3. Rub spice mixture over the pork ribs then toss ribs with sauce mixture.
4. Add pork ribs and water to the instant pot.
5. Seal pot with lid and cook on high for 30 minutes.

6. Release pressure using quick release method than open the lid.
7. Preheat the broiler. Place ribs on a baking tray and top with remaining BBQ sauce and broil for 3-5 minutes.
8. Serve and enjoy.

Nutritional Values per serving:

Calories: 694; Carbohydrates: 18.1g; Protein: 60.4g; Fat: 40.4g; Sugar: 12.9g; Sodium: 847mg

BBQ Pulled Pork

Servings: 4

Cooking Time: 15 minutes

Ingredients:

- 2 lbs pork shoulder, boneless and cut into chunks
- 1 cup beer
- 1 tbsp vinegar
- ¾ cup BBQ sauce
- 1/8 tsp cayenne pepper
- 1 tsp black pepper
- ¼ tsp oregano
- ½ tsp onion powder
- 1 tsp ground cumin
- 2 tsp chili powder
- 2 tsp paprika
- 1 tbsp brown sugar
- 1 tsp sea salt

Directions:

1. In a small bowl, mix together all the spice.
2. Add meat in a large bowl. Rub spice mixture all over the meat.
3. Pour vinegar and BBQ sauce over the meat and stir well.

4. Add beer and meat mixture into the instant pot.
5. Seal pot with lid and cook on high for 15 minutes.
6. Release pressure using quick release method than open the lid.
7. Shred the meat using a fork and serve.

Nutritional Values per serving:

Calories: 779; Carbohydrates: 23.5g; Protein: 53.6g; Fat: 49.2g; Sugar: 14.8g; Sodium: 1165mg

Pork Chops with Gravy

Servings: 4

Cooking Time: 18 minutes

Ingredients:

- 2 ½ lbs pork chops
- 1 tbsp cornstarch
- 2 tbsp water
- 1 cup chicken stock
- ½ tsp thyme
- 2 tbsp dried onion, minced
- 3 garlic cloves, smashed
- ¼ cup dry white wine
- 2 onions, sliced
- 2 tbsp olive oil
- Pepper
- Salt

Directions:

1. Season meat with pepper and salt and set aside.
2. Add oil into the instant pot and set the pot on sauté mode.
3. Add onion to the pot and sauté for 10 minutes.
4. Add garlic and wine and stir well.

5. Add thyme and dried onion. Add seasoned pork chops with stock. Stir well to combine.
6. Seal pot with lid and cook on high for 8 minutes.
7. Allow to release pressure naturally than open the lid.
8. Remove pork chops from pot and place on a plate.
9. In a small bowl, mix together cornstarch and water and pour into the instant pot and cook on sauté mode until gravy thickens.
10. Pour gravy over pork chops and serve.

Nutritional Values per serving:

Calories: 636; Carbohydrates: 3.9g; Protein: 88.7g; Fat: 26.1g; Sugar: 0.6g; Sodium: 390mg

Spicy & Smoky Beef

Servings: 4

Cooking Time: 15 minutes

Ingredients:

- 1 ¾ lbs flank steak, cut into strips
- ½ cup chicken stock
- ½ cup tomato sauce
- 1 onion, sliced
- 2 bell peppers, sliced
- ½ tsp oregano
- 1 tsp paprika
- 1 chipotle pepper in adobo sauce
- 3 garlic cloves, minced
- 2 tbsp olive oil
- Pepper
- Salt

Directions:

1. Season meat with pepper and salt.
2. Add oil into the instant pot and set the pot on sauté mode.
3. Add meat to the pot and sauté until brown.
4. Add remaining ingredients into the pot and stir well to combine.

5. Seal pot with lid and cook on high for 15 minutes.
6. Allow to release pressure naturally then open the lid.
7. Shred the meat using a fork and serve,

Nutritional Values per serving:

Calories: 492; Carbohydrates: 10.2g; Protein: 57.1g; Fat: 24.2g; Sugar: 5.6g; Sodium: 490mg

Coconut Beef Curry

Servings: 4

Cooking Time: 15 minutes

Ingredients:

- 1 ½ lbs beef, boneless and cut into chunks
- ½ cup basil, sliced
- 2 tbsp brown sugar
- 2 tbsp fish sauce
- ¼ cup chicken stock
- ¾ cup coconut milk
- 2 tbsp curry paste
- 1 onion, sliced
- 1 bell pepper, sliced
- 1 sweet potato, peeled and cut into chunks

Directions:

1. Add all ingredients except basil into the instant pot and stir well.
2. Seal pot with lid and cook on high for 15 minutes.
3. Allow to release pressure naturally then open the lid.
4. Add basil and stir well.
5. Serve over rice and enjoy.
6. Nutritional Values per serving:
7. Calories: 538; Carbohydrates: 20.2g; Protein: 54.8g; Fat: 25.9g; Sugar: 10.8g; Sodium: 875mg

Classic Sirloin Tips with Gravy

Servings: 4

Cooking Time: 10 minutes

Ingredients:

- 1 ½ lbs beef tips
- 1 tbsp cornstarch
- 2 tbsp water
- 1 cup chicken stock
- ¼ cup dry sherry
- 1 ½ tsp thyme
- 2 tbsp dried onion, minced
- 8 oz mushrooms, sliced
- 2 onions, sliced
- Pepper
- Salt

Directions:

1. In a small bowl, mix together cornstarch and water. Set aside
2. Season meat with pepper and salt.
3. Add meat to the pot along with remaining ingredients and stir well.
4. Seal pot with lid and cook on high for 10 minutes.
5. Allow to release pressure naturally then open the lid.

6. Remove meat from pot and place on a dish.
7. Add cornstarch mixture to the pot and cook on sauté mode until gravy thickens.
8. Return meat to the pot and stir well.
9. Serve and enjoy.

Nutritional Values per serving:

Calories: 426; Carbohydrates: 5.3g; Protein: 47.9g; Fat: 22.9g; Sugar: 1.7g; Sodium: 341mg

Moist & Tender Chuck Roast

Servings: 6

Cooking Time: 20 minutes

Ingredients:

- 3 lbs beef chuck roast, boneless and cut into chunks
- 2 tbsp parsley, chopped
- ½ cup red wine
- ½ cup chicken stock
- 1 tbsp soy sauce
- 2 tbsp tomato paste
- ½ tsp thyme
- 3 garlic cloves, crushed
- 2 celery ribs, chopped
- 2 carrots, peeled and sliced
- 2 onions, chopped
- Pepper
- Salt

Directions:

1. Season meat with pepper and salt and set aside.
2. Add onions, wine, stock, soy sauce, tomato paste, thyme, garlic, celery, carrots, pepper and salt to the pot and stir well. Place meat on top.
3. Seal pot with lid and cook on high for 20 minutes.

4. Allow to release pressure naturally then open the lid.
5. Shred the meat using a fork.
6. Add parsley and stir well.
7. Serve and enjoy.

Nutritional Values per serving:

Calories: 872; Carbohydrates: 7.9g; Protein: 60.5g; Fat: 63.3g; Sugar: 3.5g; Sodium: 409mg

Honey Pork Roast

Servings: 2

Cooking Time: 35 minutes

Ingredients:

- 1 lb pork roast
- 1 tbsp soy sauce
- 2 tbsp grated parmesan cheese
- ½ tbsp olive oil
- ½ tbsp garlic, minced
- ½ cup chicken stock
- ½ tbsp cornstarch
- ½ tbsp basil
- 2 tbsp honey
- Salt

Directions:

1. Add all ingredients into the instant pot and stir well.
2. Seal pot with lid and cook on meat mode for 35 minutes.
3. Allow to release pressure naturally than open the lid.
4. Stir well and serve warm.

Nutritional Values per serving:

Calories: 618; Carbohydrates: 20.6g; Protein: 68.5g; Fat: 27.3g; Sugar: 17.6g; Sodium: 968mg

Simple Meatballs

Servings: 2

Cooking Time: 25 minutes

Ingredients:

- 1 egg
- ¼ cup onion, chopped
- ¾ lb ground pork
- ¾ tsp brown sugar
- ¼ cup coconut milk
- 1 tbsp breadcrumbs

Directions:

1. In a bowl, combine together meat, breadcrumbs, and egg.
2. Make small balls from meat mixture.
3. Add coconut milk and prepared meatballs into the instant pot.
4. Add onion and brown sugar and stir well.
5. Seal pot with lid and cook on high for 25 minutes.
6. Allow to release pressure naturally then open the lid.
7. Serve warm and enjoy.

Nutritional Values per serving:

Calories: 367; Carbohydrates: 6.7g; Protein: 48.6g; Fat: 15.5g; Sugar: 3.1g; Sodium: 158mg

Shredded Thyme Pork

Servings: 3

Cooking Time: 40 minutes

Ingredients:

- 1 lb pork belly, cut into cubes
- 1 tsp thyme
- 1 ½ tsp black pepper
- ½ cup onion, chopped
- ½ cup chicken stock
- 3 tbsp water
- 1 tbsp cornstarch
- ¼ tsp salt

Directions:

1. In a small bowl, mix together cornstarch and water and set aside.
2. Add remaining ingredients to the instant pot and stir well.
3. Seal pot with lid and cook on high for 35 minutes.
4. Release pressure using quick release method than open the lid.
5. Pour cornstarch mixture into the instant pot and stir well.
6. Serve and enjoy.

Nutritional Values per serving:

Calories: 654; Carbohydrates: 7.2g; Protein: 19.6g; Fat: 60.2g; Sugar: 1g; Sodium: 1324mg

Pineapple Cinnamon Pork

Servings: 2

Cooking Time: 25 minutes

Ingredients:

- ½ lb pork tenderloin, sliced
- ½ cup tomato puree
- ½ tsp rosemary
- ¼ cup onion, chopped
- 2 cloves
- ½ tsp cinnamon
- ½ tsp nutmeg
- ½ cup pineapple, cut into chunks
- 1 cup pineapple juice

Directions:

1. Add all ingredients except pineapple into the instant pot and stir well.
2. Seal pot with lid and cook on high for 25 minutes.
3. Release pressure using quick release method than open the lid.
4. Add pineapple chunks and stir well.
5. Serve and enjoy.

Nutritional Values per serving:

Calories: 284; Carbohydrates: 29.4g; Protein: 31.6g; Fat: 4.6g; Sugar: 20.3g; Sodium: 86mg

Superb Banana Dessert

Preparation time: 10 minutes

Cooking time: 30 minutes

Servings: 4

Ingredients:

- Juice from ½ lemon
- 2 tablespoons stevia
- 3 ounces water
- 1 tablespoon coconut oil
- 4 bananas, peeled and sliced
- ½ teaspoon cardamom seeds

Directions:

1. Put bananas, stevia, water, oil, lemon juice and cardamom in your instant pot, stir a bit, cover and cook on High for 30 minutes, shaking the pot from time to time.
2. Divide into bowls and serve.
3. Enjoy!

Nutritional Values per serving: Calories 87, fat 1, fiber 2, carbs 3, protein 3

Rhubarb Dessert

Preparation time: 10 minutes

Cooking time: 5 minutes

Servings: 4

Ingredients:

- 5 cups rhubarb, chopped
- 2 tablespoons ghee, melted
- 1/3 cup water
- 1 tablespoon stevia
- 1 teaspoon vanilla extract

Directions:

1. Put rhubarb, ghee, water, stevia and vanilla extract in your instant pot, cover and cook on High for 5 minutes.
2. Divide into small bowls and serve cold.
3. Enjoy!

Nutritional Values per serving: Calories 83, fat 2, fiber 1, carbs 2, protein 2

Plum Delight

Preparation time: 10 minutes

Cooking time: 5 minutes

Servings: 10

Ingredients:

- 4 pounds plums, stones removed and chopped
- 1 cup water
- 2 tablespoons stevia
- 1 teaspoon cinnamon, powder
- ½ teaspoon cardamom, ground

Directions:

1. Put plums, water, stevia, cinnamon and cardamom in your instant pot, cover and cook on High for 5 minutes.
2. Stir well, pulse a bit using an immersion blender, divide into small jars and serve.
3. Enjoy!

Nutritional Values per serving: Calories 83, fat 0, fiber 1, carbs 2, protein 5

Refreshing Fruits Dish

Preparation time: 10 minutes

Cooking time: 10 minutes

Servings: 4

Ingredients:

- 1 and ½ pounds plums, stones removed and halved
- 2 tablespoons stevia
- 1 tablespoon cinnamon powder
- 2 apples, cored, peeled and cut into wedges
- 2 tablespoons lemon zest, grated
- 2 teaspoons balsamic vinegar
- 1 cup hot water

Directions:

- Put plums, water, apples, stevia, cinnamon, lemon zest and vinegar in your instant pot, cover and cook on High for 10 minutes.
- Stir again well, divide into small cups and serve cold.

Nutritional Values per serving: Calories 73, fat 0, fiber 1, carbs 2, protein 4

Dessert Stew

Preparation time: 10 minutes

Cooking time: 6 minutes

Servings: 6

Ingredients:

- 14 plums, stones removed and halved
- 2 tablespoons stevia
- 1 teaspoon cinnamon powder
- ¼ cup water
- 2 tablespoons arrowroot powder

Directions:

1. Put plums, stevia, cinnamon, water and arrowroot in your instant pot, cover and cook on High for 6 minutes.
2. Divide into small jars and serve cold.
3. Enjoy!

Nutritional Values per serving: Calories 83, fat 0, fiber 1, carbs 2, protein 2

Original Fruits Dessert

Preparation time: 10 minutes

Cooking time: 10 minutes

Servings: 10

Ingredients:

- 3 cups canned pineapple chunks, drained
- 3 cups canned cherries, drained
- 2 cups canned apricots, halved and drained
- 2 cups canned peach slices, drained
- 3 cups natural applesauce
- 2 cups canned mandarin oranges, drained
- 2 tablespoons stevia
- 1 teaspoon cinnamon powder

Directions:

1. Put pineapples, cherries, apricots, peaches, applesauce, oranges, cinnamon and stevia in your instant pot, cover and cook on High for 10 minutes.
2. Divide into small bowls and serve cold.
3. Enjoy!

Nutritional Values per serving: Calories 120, fat 1, fiber 2, carbs 3, protein 2

Delicious Apples and Cinnamon

Preparation time: 10 minutes

Cooking time: 10 minutes

Servings: 8

Ingredients:

- 1 teaspoon cinnamon powder
- 12 ounces apples, cored and chopped
- 2 tablespoons flax seed meal mixed with 1 tablespoon water
- ½ cup coconut cream
- 3 tablespoons stevia
- ½ teaspoon nutmeg
- 2 teaspoons vanilla extract
- 1/3 cup pecans, chopped

Directions:

1. In your instant pot, mix flax seed meal with coconut cream, vanilla, nutmeg, stevia, apples and cinnamon, stir a bit, cover and cook on High for 10 minutes.
2. Divide into bowls, sprinkle pecans on top and serve.
3. Enjoy!

Nutritional Values per serving: Calories 120, fat 3, fiber 2, carbs 3, protein 3

Crazy Delicious Pudding

Preparation time: 10 minutes

Cooking time: 35 minutes

Servings: 6

Ingredients:

- 1 mandarin, sliced
- Juice from 2 mandarins
- 3 tablespoons stevia
- 4 ounces ghee, melted
- ½ cup water
- 2 tablespoons flax meal
- ¾ cup coconut flour
- 1 teaspoon baking powder
- ¾ cup almonds, ground

- Olive oil cooking spray

Directions:

1. Grease a loaf pan, arrange sliced mandarin on the bottom and leave aside.
2. In a bowl, mix ghee with stevia, flax meal, almonds, mandarin juice, flour and baking powder, stir and spread this over mandarin slices.
3. Add the water to your instant pot, place the trivet on top, add loaf pan, cover and cook on High for 35 minutes.
4. Leave aside to cool down, slice and serve.
5. Enjoy!

Nutritional Values per serving: Calories 200, fat 2, fiber 2, carbs 3, protein 4

Wonderful Berry Pudding

Preparation time: 10 minutes

Cooking time: 35 minutes

Servings: 6

Ingredients:

- 1 cup almond flour
- 2 tablespoons lemon juice
- 2 cups blueberries
- 2 teaspoons baking powder
- ½ teaspoon nutmeg, ground
- ½ cup coconut milk
- 3 tablespoons stevia
- 1 tablespoon flax meal mixed with 1 tablespoon water
- 3 tablespoons ghee, melted
- 1 teaspoon vanilla extract
- 1 tablespoon arrowroot powder
- 1 cup cold water

Directions:

- In a greased heat proof dish, mix blueberries and lemon juice, toss a bit and spread on the bottom.
- In a bowl, mix flour with nutmeg, stevia, baking powder, vanilla, ghee, flaxseed meal, arrowroot and milk, stir well again and spread over blueberries.
- Put the water in your instant pot, add the trivet, and the heatproof dish, cover and cook on High for 35 minutes.
- Leave pudding to cool down, transfer to dessert bowls and serve.
- Enjoy!

Nutritional Values per serving: Calories 220, fat 4, fiber 4, carbs 9, protein 6

Winter Fruits Dessert

Preparation time: 10 minutes

Cooking time: 15 minutes

Servings: 6

Ingredients:

- 1-quart water
- 2 tablespoons stevia
- 1 pound mixed apples, pears and cranberries
- 5-star anise
- A pinch of cloves, ground
- 2 cinnamon sticks
- Zest from 1 orange, grated
- Zest from 1 lemon, grated

Directions:

1. Put the water, stevia, apples, pears, cranberries, star anise, cinnamon, orange and lemon zest and cloves in your instant pot, cover and cook on High for 15 minutes.
2. Serve cold.
3. Enjoy!

Nutritional Values per serving: Calories 98, fat 0, fiber 0, carbs 0, protein 2

Different Dessert

Preparation time: 10 minutes

Cooking time: 4 minutes

Servings: 2

Ingredients:

- 2 cups orange juice
- 4 pears, peeled, cored and cut into medium chunks
- 5 cardamom pods
- 2 tablespoons stevia
- 1 cinnamon stick
- 1 small ginger piece, grated

Directions:

1. Place pears, cardamom, orange juice, stevia, cinnamon and ginger in your instant pot, cover and cook on High for 4 minutes.
2. Divide into small bowls and serve cold.
3. Enjoy!

Nutritional Values per serving: Calories 100, fat 0, fiber 1, carbs 1, protein 2

Orange Dessert

Preparation time: 10 minutes

Cooking time: 30 minutes

Servings: 4

Ingredients:

- 1 and ¾ cup water
- 1 teaspoon baking powder
- 1 cup coconut flour
- 2 tablespoons stevia
- ½ teaspoon cinnamon powder
- 3 tablespoons coconut oil, melted
- ½ cup coconut milk
- ½ cup pecans, chopped
- ½ cup raisins
- ½ cup orange peel, grated
- ¾ cup orange juice

Directions:

1. In a bowl, mix flour with stevia, baking powder, cinnamon, 2 tablespoons oil, milk, pecans and raisins, stir and transfer to a greased heat proof dish.
2. Heat up a small pan over medium high heat, mix ¾ cup water with orange juice, orange peel and the rest of the oil, stir, bring to a boil and pour over the pecans mix.
3. Put 1 cup water in your instant pot, add the trivet, add heat proof dish, cover and cook on High for 30 minutes.
4. Serve cold.
5. Enjoy!

Nutritional Values per serving: Calories 142, fat 3, fiber 1, carbs 3, protein 3

Great Pumpkin Dessert

Preparation time: 10 minutes

Cooking time: 30 minutes

Servings: 10

Ingredients:

- 1 and ½ teaspoons baking powder
- 2 cups coconut flour
- ½ teaspoon baking soda
- ¼ teaspoon nutmeg, ground
- 1 teaspoons cinnamon powder
- ¼ teaspoon ginger, grated
- 1 tablespoon coconut oil, melted
- 1 egg white
- 1 tablespoon vanilla extract
- 1 cup pumpkin puree
- 2 tablespoons stevia
- 1 teaspoon lemon juice
- 1 cup water

Directions:

1. In a bowl, flour with baking powder, baking soda, cinnamon, ginger, nutmeg, oil, egg white, ghee, vanilla extract, pumpkin puree, stevia and lemon juice, stir well and transfer this to a greased cake pan.
2. Put the water in your instant pot, add trivet, add cake pan, cover and cook on High for 30 minutes.
3. Leave cake to cool down, slice and serve.
4. Enjoy!

Nutritional Values per serving: Calories 180, fat 3, fiber 2, carbs 3, protein 4

Delicious Baked Apples

Servings: 6

Cooking Time: 14 minutes

Ingredients:

- 6 apples, cored and cut into wedges
- ¼ tsp nutmeg
- 1 tsp cinnamon
- 1/3 cup honey
- 1 cup red wine
- ¼ cup pecans, chopped
- ¼ cup raisins

Directions:

1. Add all ingredients into the instant pot and stir well.
2. Seal pot with lid and cook on manual mode for 4 minutes.
3. Allow to release pressure naturally for 10 minutes then release using quick release method.
4. Stir well and serve.

Nutritional Values per serving:

Calories: 233; Carbohydrates: 52.7g; Protein: 1g; Fat: 1.3g; Sugar: 42.6g; Sodium: 5mg

Moist Pumpkin Brownie

Servings: 16

Cooking Time: 40 minutes

Ingredients:

- 3 eggs
- 1 tsp pumpkin pie spice
- ¾ cup cocoa powder
- ¼ cup palm sugar
- ¼ cup maple syrup
- ½ cup pumpkin puree
- ¼ cup coconut oil
- Pinch of salt

Directions:

1. Spray baking dish with cooking spray and set aside.
2. Add all ingredients into the large bowl and stir well to combine. Pour batter into the prepared baking dish.
3. Pour 1 cup of water into the instant pot than place trivet in the pot.
4. Place baking dish on top of the trivet.
5. Seal pot with lid and cook on high for 4o minutes.
6. Release pressure using quick release method than open the lid.
7. Remove dish from the pot and set aside to cool completely.
8. Cut into pieces and serve.

Nutritional Values per serving:

Calories: 77; Carbohydrates: 9.3g; Protein: 1.9g; Fat: 4.8g; Sugar: 5.6g; Sodium: 32mg

Lemon Custard

Servings: 4

Cooking Time: 11 minutes

Ingredients:

- 4 eggs
- 1 tsp lemon extract
- 2/3 cup sugar
- 2 tsp lemon zest
- 2 ½ cups milk

Directions:

1. In a saucepan, add lemon zest and milk and heat over medium heat. Bring to boil and stir constantly.
2. Once milk starts to boil up then remove from heat. Set aside to cool for 15 minutes.
3. Pour milk through a strainer into a bowl.
4. In another bowl beat together eggs, lemon extract for 2-3 minutes.
5. Slowly pour milk to the egg mixture and mix until smooth and creamy.
6. Pour mixture into the 4 ramekins and cover each with foil.
7. Pour 2 cups of water into the instant pot than place trivet in the pot.

8. Place ramekins on top of the trivet.
9. Seal pot with lid and cook on high for 8 minutes.
10. Release pressure using quick release method than open the lid.
11. Remove ramekins from the pot and set aside to cool completely.
12. Place custard ramekins in the refrigerator for 2 hours.
13. Serve chilled and enjoy.

Nutritional Values per serving:

Calories: 268; Carbohydrates: 41.5g; Protein: 10.6g; Fat: 7.5g; Sugar: 40.7g; Sodium: 134mg

Pumpkin Pudding

Servings: 4

Cooking Time: 14 minutes

Ingredients:

- 4 cups pumpkin, cubed
- 1 tbsp raisins
- ½ tsp cardamom powder
- ½ cup desiccated coconut
- 10 tbsp brown sugar
- ½ cup almond milk
- 2 tbsp ghee

Directions:

1. Add ghee into the instant pot and set the pot on sauté mode.
2. Add pumpkin and sauté for 2-3 minutes. Add almond milk and stir well.
3. Seal pot with lid and cook on high for 5 minutes.
4. Release pressure using quick release method than open the lid.
5. Mash the pumpkin using the potato masher.
6. Add sugar and cook on sauté mode for 2-3 minutes.
7. Add remaining ingredients and stir well to combine and cook for 2-3 minutes.
8. Serve warm and enjoy.

Nutritional Values per serving:

Calories: 301; Carbohydrates: 14.2g; Protein: 3.5g; Fat: 14.2g; Sugar: 32.3g; Sodium: 23mg

Easy Yogurt Custard

Servings: 6

Cooking Time: 40 minutes

Ingredients:

- 1 cup Greek yogurt
- 2 tsp cardamom powder
- 1 cup milk
- 1 cup condensed milk

Directions:

1. Add all ingredients into the heat-safe bowl and mix until well combined. Cover bowl with foil.
2. Pour 2 cups of water into the instant pot than place trivet in the pot.
3. Place bowl on top of the trivet. Seal pot with lid and cook on high for 20 minutes.
4. Allow to release pressure naturally for 20 minutes then release using quick release method.
5. Remove bowl from the pot and set aside to cool completely.
6. Place custard bowl in refrigerator for 1 hour.
7. Serve chilled and enjoy.

Nutritional Values per serving:

Calories: 215; Carbohydrates: 33.1g; Protein: 7.8g; Fat: 5.8g; Sugar: 32.4g; Sodium: 113mg

Zucchini Pudding

Servings: 4

Cooking Time: 20 minutes

Ingredients:

- 2 cups zucchini, shredded
- ½ tsp cardamom powder
- 1/3 cup sugar
- 5 oz half and half
- 5 oz milk

Directions:

1. Add all ingredients except cardamom to the instant pot and stir well.
2. Seal pot with lid and cook on high for 10 minutes.
3. Allow to release pressure naturally for 10 minutes then release using quick release method.
4. Add cardamom and stir well.
5. Serve and enjoy.

Nutritional Values per serving:

Calories: 136; Carbohydrates: 22g; Protein: 2.9g; Fat: 4.9g; Sugar: 19.3g; Sodium: 37mg

Delicious Pina Colada

Servings: 8

Cooking Time: 12 minutes

Ingredients:

- 1 cup Arborio rice
- 1 tbsp cinnamon
- 5 oz can pineapple, crushed
- oz coconut milk
- 1 cup condensed milk
- 1 ½ cups water

Directions:

1. Add rice and water into the instant pot and stir well.
2. Seal pot with lid and cook on low for 12 minutes.
3. Release pressure using quick release method than open the lid.
4. Add remaining ingredients and stir well.
5. Serve and enjoy.

Nutritional Values per serving:

Calories: 330; Carbohydrates: 45.4g; Protein: 5.8g; Fat: 14.9g; Sugar: 24.2g; Sodium: 59mg

Apple Caramel Cake

Servings: 8

Cooking Time: 35 minutes

Ingredients:

- 21 oz apple fruit filling
- ¼ cup caramel syrup
- ½ cup butter, cut into slices
- 15 oz yellow cake mix

Directions:

1. Spray baking dish with cooking spray. Spread apple fruit filling in the bottom of baking dish.
2. Add caramel syrup and stir to coat.
3. Top with yellow cake mix and butter slices.
4. Pour 1 cup of water into the instant pot than place trivet in the pot.
5. Place baking dish on top of the trivet.
6. Seal pot with lid and cook on high for 35 minutes.
7. Release pressure using quick release method than open the lid.
8. Serve and enjoy.

Nutritional Values per serving:

Calories: 357; Carbohydrates: 57g; Protein: 2g; Fat: 13g; Sugar: 28g; Sodium: 596mg

Apple Rice Pudding

Servings: 8

Cooking Time: 15 minutes

Ingredients:

- ¾ cup Arborio rice
- 1 tsp cinnamon
- 1 cinnamon stick
- 1 tsp vanilla
- ¼ apple, peeled and chopped
- 2 rhubarb stalks, chopped
- ½ cup water
- 1 ½ cup milk

Directions:

1. Add all ingredients into the instant pot and stir well.
2. Seal pot with lid and cook on manual mode for 15 minutes.
3. Release pressure using quick release method than open the lid.
4. Stir well and serve.

Nutritional Values per serving:

Calories: 96; Carbohydrates: 18.3g; Protein: 2.8g; Fat: 1.1g; Sugar: 3g; Sodium: 24mg

Vegan Coconut Risotto Pudding

Servings: 6

Cooking Time: 30 minutes

Ingredients:

- ¾ cup Arborio rice
- ¼ cup maple syrup
- 1 ½ cups water
- ½ cup shredded coconut
- 1 tsp lemon juice
- ½ tsp vanilla
- 15 oz can coconut milk

Directions:

1. Add all ingredients into the instant pot and stir well.
2. Seal pot with lid and cook on manual mode for 20 minutes.
3. Allow to release pressure naturally for 10 minutes then release using quick release method.
4. Stir well and using blender blend pudding until smooth.
5. Serve and enjoy.

Nutritional Values per serving:

Calories: 284; Carbohydrates: 30.8g; Protein: 3.3g; Fat: 17.5g; Sugar: 8.3g; Sodium: 15mg

Vanilla Avocado Pudding

Servings: 2

Cooking Time: 3 minutes

Ingredients:

- 1/2 avocado, cut into cubes
- 1 tsp agar powder
- 1/4 cup coconut cream
- 1 cup coconut milk
- 2 tsp swerve
- 1 tsp vanilla

Directions:

1. Add coconut cream and avocado into the blender and blend until smooth. Set aside.
2. In a large bowl, whisk together coconut milk, vanilla, swerve, and agar powder. Stir until well combined.
3. Add coconut cream and avocado mixture and stir well.
4. Pour mixture into a heat-safe bowl.
5. Pour one cup of water into the instant pot then place a trivet in the pot.
6. Place bowl on top of the trivet.
7. Seal pot with lid and cook on steam mode for 3 minutes.

8. Release pressure using quick release method than open the lid.
9. Remove bowl from the pot and set aside to cool completely.
10. Place bowl in refrigerator for 1 hour.
11. Serve and enjoy.

Nutritional Values per serving:

Calories: 308; Carbohydrates: 27.9g; Protein: 2.1g; Fat: 21.8g; Sugar: 19.6g; Sodium: 32mg

Vanilla Almond Risotto

Servings: 4

Cooking Time: 15 minutes

Ingredients:

- 1 cup Arborio rice
- 1 cup coconut milk
- 2 cups unsweetened almond milk
- 1/4 cup sliced almonds
- 2 tsp vanilla extract
- 1/3 cup sugar

Directions:

1. Add almonds and coconut milk into the instant pot and stir well.
2. Seal pot with lid and cook on high for 5 minutes.
3. Allow to release pressure naturally for 10 minutes then release using quick release method.
4. Stir in vanilla extract and sweetener.
5. Serve and enjoy.

Nutritional Values per serving:

Calories: 432; Carbohydrates: 60.3g; Protein: 6.3g; Fat: 19.3g; Sugar: 19.2g; Sodium: 102mg

Coconut Raspberry Curd

Preparation Time: 20 minutes + chilling time

Servings 4

Nutritional Values per serving: 334 Calories; 32.9g Fat; 6.6g Total Carbs; 2.9g Protein; 3.6g Sugars

Ingredients

- 4 ounces coconut oil, softened
- 3/4 cup Swerve
- 4 egg yolks, beaten
- 1/2 cup blueberries
- 1 teaspoon grated lemon zest
- 1/2 teaspoon vanilla extract
- 1/2 teaspoon star anise, ground

Directions

1. Blend the coconut oil and Swerve in a food processor.
2. Gradually mix in the eggs; continue to blend for 1 minute longer.
3. Now, add blueberries, lemon zest, vanilla, and star anise. Divide the mixture among four Mason jars and cover them with lids.
4. Add 1 ½ cups of water and a metal rack to the Instant Pot. Now, lower your jars onto the rack.

5. Secure the lid. Choose "Manual" mode and High pressure; cook for 15 minutes. Once cooking is complete, use a natural pressure release; carefully remove the lid. Serve
6. Place in your refrigerator until ready to serve. Bon appétit!

Simple Chocolate Mousse

Preparation Time: 20 minutes + chilling time

Servings 6

Nutritional Values per serving: 205 Calories; 18.3g Fat; 5.2g Total Carbs; 3.2g Protein; 2.6g Sugars

Ingredients

- 1 cup full-fat milk
- 1 cup heavy cream
- 4 egg yolks, beaten
- 1/3 cup sugar
- 1/4 teaspoon grated nutmeg
- 1/4 teaspoon ground cinnamon
- 1/4 cup unsweetened cocoa powder

Directions

1. In a small pan, bring the milk and cream to a simmer.
2. In a mixing dish, thoroughly combine the remaining ingredients. Add this egg mixture to the warm milk mixture.
3. Pour the mixture into ramekins.
4. Add 1 ½ cups of water and a metal rack to the Instant Pot. Now, lower your ramekins onto the rack.
5. Secure the lid. Choose "Manual" mode and High pressure; cook for 10 minutes. Once cooking is complete, use a natural pressure release; carefully remove the lid. Serve
6. Serve well chilled and enjoy!

The Best Tropical Dessert Ever

Preparation Time: 15 minutes + chilling time

Servings 4

Nutritional Values per serving: 118 Calories; 8.2g Fat; 6.6g Total Carbs; 3.7g Protein; 2.6g Sugars

Ingredients

- 3 egg yolks, well whisked
- 1/3 cup Swerve
- 1/4 cup water
- 3 tablespoons cacao powder, unsweetened
- 3/4 cup whipping cream
- 1/3 cup coconut milk
- 1/4 cup shredded coconut
- 1 teaspoon vanilla essence
- A pinch of grated nutmeg
- A pinch of salt

Directions

1. Place the egg in a mixing bowl.
2. In a pan, heat the Swerve, water and cacao powder and whisk well to combine.
3. Now, stir in the whipping cream and milk; cook until heated through. Add shredded coconut, vanilla, nutmeg, and salt.
4. Now, slowly and gradually pour the chocolate mixture into the bowl with egg yolks. Stir to combine well and pour into ramekins.
5. Add 1 ½ cups of water and a metal rack to the Instant Pot. Now, lower your ramekins onto the rack.
6. Secure the lid. Choose "Manual" mode and High pressure; cook for 8 minutes. Once cooking is complete, use a quick pressure release; carefully remove the lid.
7. Place in your refrigerator until ready to serve. Bon appétit!

Crème with Almond and Chocolate

Preparation Time: 15 minutes

Servings 4

Nutritional Values per serving: 401 Calories; 37.1g Fat; 5.2g Total Carbs; 9.1g Protein; 1.7g Sugars

Ingredients

- 2 cups heavy whipping cream
- 1/2 cup water
- 4 eggs
- 1/3 cup Swerve
- 1 teaspoon almond extract
- 1 teaspoon vanilla extract
- 1/3 cup almonds, ground
- 2 tablespoons coconut oil, room temperature
- 4 tablespoons cacao powder
- 2 tablespoons gelatin

Directions

1. Start by adding 1 ½ cups of water and a metal rack to your Instant Pot.
2. Blend the cream, water, eggs, Swerve, almond extract, vanilla extract and almonds in your food processor.
3. Add the remaining ingredients and process for a minute longer.
4. Divide the mixture between four Mason jars; cover your jars with lids. Lower the jars onto the rack.
5. Secure the lid. Choose "Manual" mode and High pressure; cook for 7 minutes. Once cooking is complete, use a natural pressure release; carefully remove the lid. Bon appétit!

Cinnamon Flan

Preparation Time: 15 minutes

Servings 6

Nutritional Values per serving: 263 Calories; 21.2g Fat; 3.2g Total Carbs; 10.5g Protein; 2.8g Sugars

Ingredients

- 6 eggs
- 1 cup Swerve
- 1 ½ cups double cream
- 1/2 cup water
- 3 tablespoons dark rum
- A pinch of salt
- A pinch of freshly grated nutmeg
- 1/4 teaspoon ground cinnamon
- 1 teaspoon vanilla extract

Directions

1. Start by adding 1 ½ cups of water and a metal rack to your Instant Pot.
2. In a mixing bowl, thoroughly combine eggs and Swerve. Add double cream, water, rum, salt, nutmeg, cinnamon, and vanilla extract.
3. Pour mixture into a baking dish. Lower the dish onto the rack.
4. Secure the lid. Choose "Manual" mode and High pressure; cook for 10 minutes. Once cooking is complete, use a natural pressure release; carefully remove the lid.
5. Serve well chilled and enjoy!

Yummy Upside-Down Cake

Preparation Time: 35 minutes

Servings 5

Nutritional Values per serving: 193 Calories; 17.9g Fat; 5.1g Total Carbs; 1.2g Protein; 2.4g Sugars

Ingredients

- 1/2 pound raspberries
- 1 ½ tablespoons lemon juice
- 1 cup coconut flour
- 2 tablespoons cassava flour
- 1/2 teaspoon baking powder
- 1/8 teaspoon sea salt
- 1/4 cup coconut oil, melted
- 1 tablespoon monk fruit powder
- 1/2 teaspoon ground cinnamon
- 1/4 teaspoon grated nutmeg
- 1/2 teaspoon orange zest
- 1 teaspoon vanilla paste
- 1 ½ teaspoons powdered agar

Directions

1. Add 1 ½ cups water and a metal rack to the Instant Pot.
2. In a mixing bowl, thoroughly combine raspberries and lemon juice. Spread raspberries in the bottom of the pan.
3. In another mixing bowl, thoroughly combine coconut flour, cassava flour, baking powder, and sea salt.
4. In the third bowl, mix the coconut oil, monk fruit powder, cinnamon, nutmeg, orange zest, and vanilla. Add powdered agar and mix until everything is well incorporated.
5. Pour the liquid ingredients over dry ingredients and mix to form a dough; flatten it to form a circle.
6. Place this dough in a baking pan and cover the raspberries. Cover the pan with a sheet of aluminum foil.
7. Lower the pan onto the metal rack.
8. Secure the lid. Choose "Manual" mode and High pressure; cook for 27 minutes. Once cooking is complete, use a natural pressure release; carefully remove the lid.
9. Finally, turn the cake pan upside down and unmold it on a platter. Enjoy!

Extraordinary Chocolate Cheesecake

Preparation Time: 25 minutes + chilling time

Servings 10

Nutritional Values per serving: 351 Calories; 35.6g Fat; 4.8g Total Carbs; 4.3g Protein; 1.7g Sugars

Ingredients

- Crust:
- 1/3 cup coconut flour
- 1/3 cup almond flour
- 2 tablespoons arrowroot flour
- 2 tablespoons cocoa powder,unsweetened
- 2 tablespoons monk fruit powder
- 1/4 cup coconut oil, melted
- Filling:
- 10 ounces cream cheese, softened
- 8 ounces heavy cream, softened
- 1 teaspoon monk fruit powder
- 1/2 cup cocoa powder,unsweetened
- 3 eggs yolks, at room temperature
- 1/3 cup sour cream
- 4 ounces butter, melted
- 1/2 teaspoon vanilla essence

Directions

1. Prepare your Instant Pot by adding 1 ½ cups of water and a metal rack to its bottom.
2. Coat a bottom of a baking pan with a piece of parchment paper.
3. In mixing bowl, combine coconut flour, almond flour, arrowroot powder, 2 tablespoons of cocoa powder, and 2 tablespoons of monk fruit powder; now, stir in melted coconut oil.
4. Press the crust mixture into the bottom of the prepared baking pan.
5. To make the filling, mix the cream cheese, heavy cream, monk fruit powder, and cocoa powder.
6. Now, fold in the eggs, sour cream, butter, and vanilla; continue to blend until everything is well incorporated,
7. Lower the baking pan onto the rack. Cover with a sheet of foil, making a foil sling.
8. Secure the lid. Choose "Manual" mode and High pressure; cook for 18 minutes. Once cooking is complete, use a natural pressure release; carefully remove the lid.
9. Place this cheesecake in your refrigerator for 3 to 4 hours. Bon appétit!

Old-School Cheesecake

Preparation Time: 35 minutes + chilling time

Servings 10

Nutritional Values per serving: 188 Calories; 17.2g Fat; 4.5g Total Carbs; 5.5g Protein; 1.3g Sugars

Ingredients

- Crust:
- 1/2 cup almond flour
- 1/2 cup coconut flour
- 1 ½ tablespoons powdered erythritol
- 1/4 teaspoon kosher salt
- 3 tablespoons butter, melted
- Filling:
- 8 ounces sour cream, at room temperature
- 8 ounces cream cheese, at room temperature
- 1/2 cup powdered erythritol
- 3 tablespoons orange juice
- 1/2 teaspoon ginger powder
- 1 teaspoon vanilla extract
- 3 eggs, at room temperature

Directions

1. Line a round baking pan with a piece of parchment paper.
2. In a mixing bowl, thoroughly combine all crust ingredients in the order listed above.
3. Press the crust mixture into the bottom of the pan.
4. Then, make the filling by mixing the sour cream and cream cheese until uniform and smooth; add the remaining ingredients and continue to beat until everything is well combined.
5. Pour the cream cheese mixture over the crust. Cover with aluminum foil, making a foil sling.
6. Place 1 ½ cups of water and a metal trivet in your Instant Pot. Then, place the pan on the metal rack.
7. Secure the lid. Choose "Manual" mode and High pressure; cook for 30 minutes. Once cooking is complete, use a natural pressure release; carefully remove the lid. Serve well chilled and enjoy!

Sweet and Sour Tale Cake

Preparation Time: 25 minutes

Servings 6

Nutritional Values per serving: 173 Calories; 15.6g Fat; 2.5g Total Carbs; 6.2g Protein; 1.6g Sugars

Ingredients

- Crust:
- 3/4 cup coconut flour
- 1/4 cup coconut oil
- 2 tablespoons Swerve
- 1/2 teaspoon pure lemon extract
- 1/2 teaspoon pure coconut extract
- 1/2 teaspoon pure vanilla extract
- 1/2 teaspoon baking powder
- A pinch of grated nutmeg
- A pinch of salt
- Filling:
- 4 eggs
- 1/2 cup Swerve
- 3 tablespoons freshly squeezed lemon juice
- 3 tablespoons shredded coconut
- 1/4 teaspoon cinnamon powder

Directions

1. Start by adding 1 ½ cups of water and a metal rack to your Instant Pot. Now, spritz a baking pan with a nonstick cooking spray (butter flavor.
2. Then, thoroughly combine all crust ingredients in your food processor. Now, spread the crust mixture evenly on the bottom of the prepared pan. Do not forget to prick a few holes with a fork.
3. Lower the baking pan onto the rack.
4. Secure the lid. Choose "Manual" mode and High pressure; cook for 8 minutes. Once cooking is complete, use a quick pressure release; carefully remove the lid.
5. Meanwhile, thoroughly combine all filling ingredients in your food processor. Spread the filling mixture evenly over top of the warm crust.
6. Return to the Instant Pot.
7. Secure the lid. Choose "Manual" mode and High pressure; cook for 15 minutes. Once cooking is complete, use a quick pressure release; carefully remove the lid.
8. Cut into squares and serve at room temperature or chilled. Bon appétit!

Lazy Sunday Cake

Preparation Time: 30 minutes

Servings 6

Nutritional Values per serving: 121 Calories; 7.3g Fat; 5.9g Total Carbs; 6.5g Protein; 2.3g Sugars

Ingredients

- 1/2 cup peanut butter
- 1 pound zucchini, shredded
- 1/4 cup Swerve
- 2 eggs, beaten
- 1/2 teaspoon ground star anise
- 1 teaspoon ground cinnamon
- 1/4 teaspoon grated nutmeg
- 1/2 teaspoon rum extract
- 1/2 teaspoon vanilla
- 1/2 teaspoon baking powder

Directions

1. Start by adding 1 ½ cups of water and a metal trivet to your Instant Pot. Now, spritz a baking pan with a nonstick cooking spray.
2. In a mixing dish, thoroughly combine all ingredients until uniform, creamy and smooth. Pour the batter into the prepared pan.
3. Lower the pan onto the trivet.
4. Secure the lid. Choose "Bean/Chili" mode and High pressure; cook for 25 minutes. Once cooking is complete, use a natural pressure release; carefully remove the lid.
5. Allow your cake to cool completely before cutting and serving.Bon appétit!

Keto Chocolate Brownies

Preparation Time: 30 minutes

Servings 6

Nutritional Values per serving: 384 Calories; 36.6g Fat; 5.2g Total Carbs; 7.7g Protein; 1.3g Sugars

Ingredients

- 4 ounces chocolate, sugar-free
- 1/2 cup coconut oil
- 2 cups Swerve
- 4 eggs, whisked
- 1 teaspoon vanilla paste
- 1/4 teaspoon sea salt
- 1/4 teaspoon grated nutmeg
- 1/2 teaspoon dried lavender flowers
- 1/4 cup almond flour
- 1/2 cup whipped cream

Directions

1. Start by adding 1 ½ cups of water and a metal trivet to your Instant Pot. Now, spritz a baking pan with a nonstick cooking spray.
2. Thoroughly combine the chocolate, coconut oil, and Swerve. Gradually, whisk in the eggs. Add the vanilla paste, salt, nutmeg, lavender flowers and almond flour; mix until everything is well incorporated.
3. Secure the lid. Choose "Bean/Chili" mode and High pressure; cook for 25 minutes. Once cooking is complete, use a natural pressure release; carefully remove the lid.
4. Top with whipped cream and serve well chilled. Bon appétit!

Sweet Porridge with a Twist

Preparation Time: 10 minutes

Servings 2

Nutritional Values per serving: 363 Calories; 36.4g Fat; 6.2g Total Carbs; 4.9g Protein; 3.8g Sugars

Ingredients

- 1/2 cup coconut shreds
- 1 tablespoon sunflower seeds
- 2 tablespoons flax seeds
- 2 cardamom pods, crushed slightly
- 1 teaspoon ground cinnamon
- 1 teaspoon Stevia powdered extract
- 1 teaspoon rosewater
- 1/2 cup water
- 1 cup coconut milk

Directions

1. Add all ingredients to the Instant Pot.
2. Secure the lid. Choose "Manual" mode and High pressure; cook for 5 minutes. Once cooking is complete, use a quick pressure release; carefully remove the lid.
3. Ladle into two serving bowls and serve warm. Enjoy!

Cheesecake Tropicana

Preparation Time: 30 minutes + chilling time

Servings 5

Nutritional Values per serving: 268 Calories; 22.7g Fat; 6.6g Total Carbs; 9.5g Protein; 4.2g Sugars

Ingredients

- 9 ounces cream cheese
- 1/3 cup Swerve
- 1/2 teaspoon ginger powder
- 1 teaspoon grated orange zest
- 1 teaspoon vanilla extract
- 3 eggs
- 4 tablespoons double cream
- 1 tablespoon Swerve
- 1 navel orange, peeled and sliced

Directions

1. Start by adding 1 ½ cups of water and a metal rack to your Instant Pot. Now, spritz a baking pan with a nonstick cooking spray.
2. Beat cream cheese, 1/3 cup of Swerve, ginger, grated orange zest, and vanilla with an electric mixer.
3. Now, gradually fold in the eggs, and continue to mix until everything is well incorporated. Press this

mixture into the prepared baking pan and cover with foil.

4. Secure the lid. Choose "Bean/Chili" mode and High pressure; cook for 25 minutes. Once cooking is complete, use a natural pressure release; carefully remove the lid.
5. Mix the cream and 1 tablespoon of Swerve; spread this topping on the cake. Allow it to cool on a wire rack.
6. Then, transfer your cake to the refrigerator. Garnish with orange slices and serve well chilled. Bon appétit!

Classic Holiday Custard

Preparation Time: 20 minutes + chilling time

Servings 4

Nutritional Values per serving: 201 Calories; 17.7g Fat; 6.2g Total Carbs; 4.2g Protein; 1.2g Sugars

Ingredients

- 5 egg yolks
- 1/3 cup coconut milk, unsweetened
- 1/2 teaspoon vanilla extract
- 1 teaspoon monk fruit powder
- 1 tablespoon butterscotch flavoring
- 1/2 stick butter, melted

Directions

1. Blend the egg yolks with coconut milk, vanilla extract, monk fruit powder, and butterscotch flavoring.
2. Then, stir in the butter; stir until everything is well incorporated. Divide the mixture among four Mason jars and cover them with lids.
3. Add 1 ½ cups of water and a metal rack to the Instant Pot. Now, lower your jars onto the rack.
4. Secure the lid. Choose "Manual" mode and Low pressure; cook for 15 minutes. Once cooking is complete, use a natural pressure release; carefully remove the lid. Serve
5. Place in your refrigerator until ready to serve. Bon appétit!

Blackberry Espresso Brownies

Preparation Time: 30 minutes

Servings 8

Nutritional Values per serving: 151 Calories; 13.6g Fat; 6.7g Total Carbs; 4.1g Protein; 1.1g Sugars

Ingredients

- 4 eggs
- 1 ¼ cups coconut cream
- 1 teaspoon Stevia liquid concentrate
- 1/3 cup cocoa powder, unsweetened
- 1/2 teaspoon grated nutmeg
- 1/2 teaspoon cinnamon powder
- 1 teaspoon espresso coffee
- 1 teaspoon pure almond extract
- 1 teaspoon pure vanilla extract
- 1 teaspoon baking powder
- A pinch of kosher salt
- 1 cup blackberries, fresh or frozen (thawed

Instructions

1. Start by adding 1 ½ cups of water and a metal rack to your Instant Pot. Now, spritz a baking pan with a nonstick cooking spray.

2. Now, mix eggs, coconut cream, Stevia, cocoa powder, nutmeg, cinnamon, coffee, pure almond extract vanilla, baking powder, and salt with an electric mixer.
3. Crush the blackberries with a fork. After that, fold in your blackberries into the prepared mixture.
4. Pour the batter into the prepared pan.
5. Secure the lid. Choose "Bean/Chili" mode and High pressure; cook for 25 minutes. Once cooking is complete, use a natural pressure release; carefully remove the lid. Bon appétit!

Sweet Porridge with Blueberries

Preparation Time: 10 minutes

Servings 4

Nutritional Values per serving: 219 Calories; 18.2g Fat; 6.2g Total Carbs; 5.6g Protein; 2.9g Sugars

Ingredients

- 6 tablespoons golden flax meal
- 6 tablespoons coconut flour
- 2 cups water
- 1/4 teaspoon freshly grated nutmeg
- 1/4 teaspoon Himalayan salt
- 3 egg, whisked
- 1/2 stick butter, softened
- 4 tablespoons double cream
- 4 tablespoons monk fruit powder
- 1 cup blueberries

Directions

1. Add all ingredients to the Instant Pot.
2. Secure the lid. Choose "Manual" mode and High pressure; cook for 5 minutes. Once cooking is complete, use a quick pressure release; carefully remove the lid.
3. Serve garnished with some extra berries if desired. Enjoy!

Vanilla Berry Cupcakes

Preparation Time: 35 minutes

Servings 6

Nutritional Values per serving: 403 Calories; 42.1g Fat; 4.1g Total Carbs; 4.2g Protein; 2.1g Sugars

Ingredients

- Cupcakes:
- 1/2 cup coconut flour
- 1/2 cup almond flour
- 1/2 teaspoon baking soda
- 1 teaspoon baking powder
- A pinch of salt
- A pinch of grated nutmeg
- 1 teaspoon ginger powder
- 1 stick butter, at room temperature
- 1/2 cup Swerve
- 3 eggs, beaten
- 1/2 teaspoon pure coconut extract
- 1/2 teaspoon pure vanilla extract
- 1/2 cup double cream
- Frosting:
- 1 stick butter, at room temperature
- 1/2 cup Swerve

- 1 teaspoon pure vanilla extract
- 1/2 teaspoon coconut extract
- 6 tablespoons coconut, shredded
- 3 tablespoons raspberry, puréed
- 6 frozen raspberries

Directions

1. Start by adding 1 ½ cups of water and a rack to your Instant Pot.
2. In a mixing dish, thoroughly combine the cupcake ingredients. Divide the batter between silicone cupcake liners. Cover with a piece of foil.
3. Place the cupcakes on the rack.
4. Secure the lid. Choose "Manual" mode and High pressure; cook for 25 minutes. Once cooking is complete, use a natural pressure release; carefully remove the lid.
5. In the meantime, thoroughly combine the frosting ingredients. Put this mixture into a piping bag and top your cupcakes.
6. Garnish with frozen raspberries and enjoy!

Mini Cheesecakes with Berries

Preparation Time: 25 minutes

Servings 6

Nutritional Values per serving: 232 Calories; 22.1g Fat; 4.8g Total Carbs; 5.7g Protein; 1.9g Sugars

Ingredients

- 1/4 cup sesame seed flour
- 1/4 cup hazelnut flour
- 1/2 cup coconut flour
- 1 ½ teaspoons baking powder
- A pinch of kosher salt
- A pinch of freshly grated nutmeg
- 1/2 teaspoon ground star anise
- 1/2 teaspoon ground cinnamon
- 1/2 stick butter
- 1 cup Swerve
- 2 eggs, beaten
- 1/2 cup cream cheese
- 1/3 cup fresh mixed berries
- 1/2 vanilla paste

Directions

1. Start by adding 1 ½ cups of water and a rack to your Instant Pot.
2. In a mixing dish, thoroughly combine all of the above ingredients. Divide the batter between lightly greased ramekins. Cover with a piece of foil.
3. Place the ramekins on the rack.
4. Secure the lid. Choose "Manual" mode and High pressure; cook for 20 minutes. Once cooking is complete, use a natural pressure release; carefully remove the lid.

Special Berry Crisp with Cinnamon

Preparation Time: 15 minutes

Servings 4

Nutritional Values per serving: 255 Calories; 24.6g Fat; 5.6g Total Carbs; 3.4g Protein; 2.5g Sugars

Ingredients

- 1/2 pound blackberries
- 1 teaspoon ground cinnamon
- 1/4 teaspoon grated nutmeg
- 1/2 teaspoon ground cardamom
- 1/2 teaspoon vanilla paste
- 1/2 cup water
- 1/4 cup Swerve
- 5 tablespoons coconut oil, melted
- 1/2 cup almonds, roughly chopped
- 1/4 cup coconut flour
- 1/4 teaspoon Stevia
- A pinch of salt

Directions

1. Place blackberries on the bottom of your Instant Pot. Sprinkle with cinnamon, nutmeg, and cardamom. Add vanilla, water and Swerve.
2. In a mixing bowl, thoroughly combine the remaining ingredients. Drop by the spoonful on top of the blackberries.
3. Secure the lid. Choose "Manual" mode and High pressure; cook for 10 minutes. Once cooking is complete, use a natural pressure release; carefully remove the lid.
4. Serve at room temperature and enjoy!

Yummy Fire Cheesecake

Preparation Time: 40 minutes

Servings 6

Nutritional Values per serving: 373 Calories; 36.7g Fat; 5.1g Total Carbs; 8g Protein; 2.6g Sugars

Ingredients

- 1/2 cup almond flour
- 1/2 cup coconut flour
- 4 tablespoons coconut oil, melted
- 3/4 pound cream cheese, at room temperature
- 3/4 cup Swerve
- 3 eggs
- A pinch of salt
- A pinch of grated nutmeg
- 1/2 teaspoon ground cinnamon
- 1/2 teaspoon ground star anise
- 1 teaspoon vanilla extract
- 1 teaspoon red food coloring

Directions

1. Start by adding 1 ½ cups of water and a metal rack to your Instant Pot.

2. In a mixing bowl, thoroughly combine almond flour, coconut flour, and coconut oil. Press this mixture into a lightly greased cheesecake pan.
3. In another mixing bowl, beat the cream cheese together with Swerve. Fold in the eggs, one at a time, and continue to beat until well mixed.
4. Then, add the spices and extract; mix until everything is well incorporated. Spread the filling over the top of your cheesecake. Lower the pan onto the rack.
5. Secure the lid. Choose "Bean/Chili" mode and High pressure; cook for 35 minutes. Once cooking is complete, use a natural pressure release; carefully remove the lid. Bon appétit!

Classic Carrot Cake

Preparation Time: 35 minutes

Servings 8

Nutritional Values per serving: 381 Calories; 35.1g Fat; 4.4g Total Carbs; 10.3g Protein; 1.7g Sugars

Ingredients

- Carrot Cake:
- 2 cups carrots, grated
- 1 cup almond flour
- 1/2 cup coconut, shredded
- 1/4 cup hazelnuts, chopped
- 1/4 teaspoon ground cloves
- 1/4 teaspoon grated nutmeg
- 1/2 teaspoon ground cinnamon
- 1/2 teaspoon baking soda
- 1 teaspoon baking powder
- 4 tablespoons Swerve
- 1 teaspoon pure vanilla extract
- 4 eggs, beaten
- 1 stick butter, melted
- Cream Cheese Frosting:

1 cup cream cheese

2 tablespoons Swerve

1/2 teaspoon pure vanilla extract

Directions

1. Start by adding 1 ½ cups of water and a metal rack to your Instant Pot. Now, spritz a cheesecake pan with a nonstick cooking spray.
2. In a mixing bowl, thoroughly combine dry ingredients for the cake. Then, mix the wet ingredients until everything is well combined.
3. Pour the wet mixture into the dry mixture and stir to combine well. Spoon the batter into the cheesecake pan.
4. Cover with a sheet of foil. Lower the pan onto the rack.
5. Secure the lid. Choose "Bean/Chili" mode and High pressure; cook for 30 minutes. Once cooking is complete, use a quick pressure release; carefully remove the lid.
6. Meanwhile, mix the frosting ingredients. Frost the carrot cake and serve chilled. Enjoy!

Classic Brownie with Blackberry-Goat Cheese Swirl

Preparation Time: 30 minutes

Servings 8

Nutritional Values per serving: 309 Calories; 27.6g Fat; 3.4g Total Carbs; 10.8g Protein; 1.1g Sugars

Ingredients

- Brownies:
- 5 tablespoons coconut oil, melted
- 1 cup Swerve
- 1/4 cup cocoa powder, unsweetened
- 3 teaspoons water
- 1/2 teaspoon vanilla extract
- 3 eggs, beaten
- 1/4 cup golden flax meal
- 3/4 cup almond flour
- 1/2 teaspoon baking soda
- 1/2 teaspoon baking powder
- A pinch of salt
- A pinch of grated nutmeg
- 1/4 cup chocolate chunks, sugar-free

Blackberry Goat Cheese Swirl:

- 2 tablespoons unsalted butter, softened
- 4 ounces goat cheese, softened
- 2 ounces cream cheese, softened
- 1 cup blackberries, fresh or frozen (thawed
- 1 tablespoon Swerve
- 1/2 teaspoon almond extract
- A pinch of salt

Directions

1. Start by adding 1 ½ cups of water and a metal rack to your Instant Pot. Now, spritz a square cake pan with a nonstick cooking spray.
2. Mix the coconut oil with Swerve, cocoa powder, water, and vanilla until well combined. Mix in the eggs, flour, baking soda, baking powder, salt, and nutmeg.
3. Mix until smooth and creamy. Add the chocolate and mix one more time. Add the batter to the prepared pan.
4. Secure the lid. Choose "Manual" mode and High pressure; cook for 25 minutes. Once cooking is complete, use a quick pressure release; carefully remove the lid.
5. Invert your brownie onto a platter. Allow it to cool to room temperature.

6. Meanwhile, make the blackberry-goat cheese swirl. Beat the butter and cheese with an electric mixer; add blackberries, Swerve, almond extract and salt and continue to beat until light and fluffy.
7. Drop this mixture on top of your brownie in spoonfuls; then swirl it with a knife. Bon appétit!

Special Birthday Cake

Preparation Time: 35 minutes + chilling time

Servings 8

Nutritional Values per serving: 230 Calories; 18.8g Fat; 6.1g Total Carbs; 8.9g Protein; 1.4g Sugars

Ingredients

- Batter:
- 1 cup hazelnut flour
- 2 tablespoons arrowroot starch
- 1/2 cup cocoa powder
- 1 ¼ teaspoons baking powder
- 1/4 teaspoon kosher salt
- 1/4 teaspoon freshly grated nutmeg
- 6 eggs, whisked
- 8 tablespoons coconut oil, melted
- 1 teaspoon pure vanilla extract
- 1/2 teaspoon pure hazelnut extract
- 2/3 cup Swerve
- 1/3 cup full-fat milk
- Hazelnut Ganache:
- 1/2 cup heavy cream
- 5 ounces dark chocolate, sugar-free
- 2 tablespoons coconut oil

Directions

1. Start by adding 1 ½ cups of water and a metal rack to your Instant Pot. Now, lightly grease a baking pan with a nonstick cooking spray.
2. In a mixing bowl, thoroughly combine dry ingredients for the batter. In another bowl, mix wet ingredients for the batter.
3. Add wet mixture to the dry mixture; mix to combine well. Pour the mixture into the prepared baking pan.
4. Secure the lid. Choose "Bean/Chili" mode and High pressure; cook for 30 minutes. Once cooking is complete, use a natural pressure release; carefully remove the lid.
5. Now, place the cake pan on a wire rack until it is cool to the touch. Allow it to cool completely before frosting.
6. Meanwhile, make your ganache. In a medium pan, bring the heavy cream to a boil. Turn the heat off as soon as you see the bubbles.
7. Add chocolate and coconut oil and whisk to combine well. Frost the cake and serve well chilled.

Holiday Blueberry Pudding

Preparation Time: 20 minutes

Servings 6

Nutritional Values per serving: 240 Calories; 20.5g Fat; 5.4g Total Carbs; 4.8g Protein; 3.1g Sugars

Ingredients

- 1 cup almond flour
- 3 tablespoons sunflower seed flour
- 1/2 cup Swerve
- 1/2 teaspoon baking soda
- 1 teaspoon baking powder
- 1/4 cup coconut cream
- 1/4 cup water
- 1/4 cup coconut oil, softened
- 2 tablespoons dark rum
- 1/2 teaspoon vanilla
- 1/2 cup blueberries

Directions

1. Start by adding 1 ½ cups of water and a metal trivet to your Instant Pot.
2. Mix all ingredients, except blueberries, until everything is well incorporated. Spoon the mixture into a lightly greased baking pan.

3. Fold in blueberries and gently stir to combine. Lower the baking dish onto the trivet.
4. Secure the lid. Choose "Bean/Chili" mode and High pressure; cook for 15 minutes. Once cooking is complete, use a natural pressure release; carefully remove the lid.
5. Allow the cobbler to cool slightly before serving. Bon appétit!

Fluffy Strawberry Cake

Preparation Time: 35 MIN

Serving: 6

Ingredients:

- 2 cups almond flour
- 1 cup coconut flour
- ¼ cup unsweetened cocoa powder
- 1 tsp baking soda
- ½ tsp baking powder
- ½ tsp salt
- 1 cup unsweetened almond milk
- 3 eggs
- 2 egg whites
- 3 cups whipped cream, sugar-free
- 1 tsp stevia extract
- 2 tsp strawberry extract

Directions:

1. Line a 7-inches springform pan with some parchment paper. Set aside.
2. In a large mixing bowl, combine almond flour, coconut flour, cocoa powder, baking soda, baking powder, and salt. Mix well and gradually add milk. With a paddle attachment on, beat well on high speed. Now add eggs,

one at the time, beating constantly. Finally, add egg whites and mix until completely incorporated. Transfer the mixture to the prepared springform pan and flatten the surface with a kitchen spatula. Cover loosely with some aluminum foil.

3. Plug in your Instant Pot and pour in 1 cup of water. Set the trivet in the stainless steel insert and gently place the springform on top.
4. Seal the lid and set the steam release handle to the 'Sealing' position. Press the 'Manual' button and set the timer for 20 minutes.
5. When done, move the steam valve to the 'Venting' position to release the pressure.
6. Open the lid and carefully remove the springform pan. Place on a wire rack and cool to a room temperature.
7. Meanwhile, place whipped cream, stevia, and strawberry extract in a large bowl. Using a hand mixer, beat well until fully combined.
8. Pour the mixture over the chilled crust and refrigerate for one hour before use.

Nutritional Values per serving:

Calories 195

Total Fats 16.4g

Net Carbs: 4.2g

Protein 5.7g

Fiber: 3.8g

Chocolate Cheesecake

Preparation Time: 45 MIN

Serving: 10

Ingredients:

- 1 cup almond flour
- 1 cup coconut flour
- 1 cup unsweetened cocoa powder, divided in half
- ¼ cup swerve
- ½ cup butter
- 2 large eggs
- 4 cups cream cheese
- ¾ cup heavy cream
- 1 tsp vanilla extract
- ½ tsp stevia powder
- 2 tbsp. oil

Directions:

1. In a large bowl, combine together almond flour, coconut flour, unsweetened cocoa powder, and swerve. Mix well and transfer to a food processor along with butter and eggs. Process well and set aside.
2. Brush a 7-inches springform pan with oil and line with some parchment paper. Add the crust mixture and press well with your hands.

3. Plug in your instant pot and pour into 1 ½ cups of water. Place the trivet in the stainless steel insert and gently put the springform on top. Cover with some aluminum foil to prevent condensate dripping.
4. Seal the lid and set the steam release handle to 'Sealing' position. Press the 'Manual' button and set the timer for 15 minutes.
5. When you hear the cooker's end signal, release the pressure naturally for 10-12 minutes. Move the pressure valve to the 'Venting' position to release any remaining pressure.
6. Open the lid and gently remove the springform pan. Chill to a room temperature.
7. Place cream cheese, heavy cream, vanilla extract, and stevia powder in a blender. Pulse to combine and pour the mixture over the chilled crust.
8. Refrigerate overnight.

Nutritional Values per serving:

Calories 548

Total Fats 52g

Net Carbs: 7.4g

Protein 12g

Fiber: 6.8g

Raspberry Compote

Preparation Time: 45 MIN

Serving: 4

Ingredients:

- 2 cups raspberries
- 1 cup swerve
- 1 tsp freshly grated lemon zest
- 1 tsp vanilla extract

Directions:

1. Plug in your instant pot and press the 'Saute' button. Add raspberries, swerve, lemon zest, and vanilla extract. Stir well and pour in 1 cup of water. Cook for 5 minutes, stirring constantly.
2. Now pour in 2 more cups of water and press the 'Cancel' button. Seal the lid and set the steam release handle to the 'Sealing' position. Press the 'Manual' button and set the timer for 15 minutes on low pressure.
3. When you hear the cooker's end signal, press the 'Cancel' button and release the pressure naturally for 10-15 minutes. Move the pressure handle to the 'Venting' position to release any remaining pressure and open the lid.

4. Optionally, stir some more lemon juice and transfer to serving bowls.
5. Chill to a room temperature and refrigerate for one hour before serving.

Nutritional Values per serving:

Calories 48

Total Fats 0.5g

Net Carbs: 5g

Protein 1g

Fiber: 5.3g

Chocolate Cream

Preparation Time: 25 MIN

Serving: 4

Ingredients:

- 2 heavy cream
- ¼ cup unsweetened dark chocolate, chopped
- 3 eggs
- 1 tsp orange zest
- 1 tsp stevia powder
- 1 tsp vanilla extract
- ½ tsp salt

Directions:

1. Plug in your instant pot and press the 'Saute' button. Add heavy cream, chopped chocolate, stevia powder, vanilla extract, orange zest, and salt. Stir well and simmer until the chocolate has completely melted. Press the 'Cancel' button and crack eggs, one at the time, stirring constantly. Remove from the instant pot.
2. Transfer the mixture to 4 mason jars with loose lids.
3. Pour 2 cups of water in your instant pot and set the trivet in the stainless steel insert. Add jars and seal the lid.

4. Set the steam release handle and press the 'Manual' button. Set the timer for 10 minutes.
5. When done, perform a quick release by moving the steam valve to the 'Venting' position.
6. Open the lid and remove the jars. Chill to a room temperature and then transfer to the refrigerator.
7. Top with some whipped cream before serving.

Nutritional Values per serving:

Calories 267

Total Fats 26.2g

Net Carbs: 2.4g

Protein 5.6g

Fiber: 0.2g

Butter Pancakes

Preparation Time: 15 MIN

Serving: 6

Ingredients:

- 2 cups cream cheese
- 2 cups almond flour
- 6 large eggs
- ¼ tsp salt
- 2 tbsp. butter
- ¼ tsp ground ginger
- ½ tsp cinnamon powder

Directions:

1. In a large mixing bowl, combine cream cheese, eggs, and one tablespoon of butter. With a paddle attachment on, beat well on high speed until light and creamy. Slowly add flour beating constantly. Finally, add salt, ginger, and cinnamon. Continue to beat until fully incorporated.
2. Plug in your instant pot and press the 'Saute' button. Grease the stainless steel insert with the remaining butter and heat up.

3. Pour in about ½ cup of the batter and cook for 2-3 minutes or until golden color. Repeat the process with the remaining batter.
4. Serve warm.

Nutritional Values per serving:

Calories 432

Total Fats 40.2g

Net Carbs: 3.5g

Protein 14.2g

Fiber: 1g

Lemon Cupcakes with Blueberries

Preparation Time: 35 MIN

Serving: 6

Ingredients:

- 2 cups almond flour
- 2/3 tsp baking powder
- ¼ tsp baking soda
- ½ tsp xanthan gum
- 1 cup swerve
- 3 eggs
- 1 cup almond milk, unsweetened
- ¼ cup blueberries
- 1 tbsp. butter, softened
- 1 tbsp. coconut oil
- 1 tbsp. lemon zest, freshly grated
- 1 tsp vanilla extract

Directions:

1. Combine all dry ingredients in a large mixing bowl. Mix well and gradually add milk. Beat well on medium speed adding eggs, one at the time. Add butter, coconut oil, lemon zest, and vanilla extract. Mix until fully incorporated. Fold in blueberries and transfer to 12-cup silicone cupcake pan.

2. Plug in your instant pot and pour in 1 cup of water. Set the trivet in the stainless steel insert and place the silicone pan on top. Cover loosely with some aluminum foil and seal the lid.
3. Set the steam release handle to the 'Sealing' position and press the 'Manual' button. Set the timer for 25 minutes.
4. When done, perform a quick pressure release and open the lid. Gently remove the muffin pan from your instant pot and cool completely before serving.

Nutritional Values per serving:

Calories 223

Total Fats 20.4g

Net Carbs: 3.8g

Protein 5.9g

Fiber: 2.9g

Chocolate Brownies

Preparation Time: 30 MIN

Serving: 8

Ingredients:

- ½ cup cocoa powder, unsweetened
- ¼ cup unsweetened dark chocolate chunks
- 1 cup cream cheese
- 2 large eggs
- 3 tbsp. coconut oil
- ½ tsp salt
- ¾ cup swerve

Directions:

1. Combine cream cheese, eggs, and coconut oil in a large mixing bowl. With a paddle attachment on, beat well on medium speed until smooth. Add cocoa powder, salt, swerve, and dark chocolate chunks. Continue to beat for 2 minutes, or until fully incorporated.
2. Brush a 7-inches cake pan with some oil and line with some parchment paper. Dust the paper with some cocoa powder and pour in the batter. Flatten the surface with a kitchen spatula and loosely cover with aluminum foil.

3. Plug in your instant pot and pour in 1 cup of water. Set the steam rack at the bottom of the steel insert and place the cake pan on top.
4. Seal the lid and set the steam release to the 'Sealing' position. Select the 'Manual' mode and set the timer for 20 minutes.
5. When you hear the cooker's end signal, release the pressure naturally for 15 minutes. Open the lid and carefully remove the pan.
6. Cool completely and cut into 8 brownies.

Nutritional Values per serving:

Calories 180

Total Fats 17.5g

Net Carbs: 2.4g

Protein 4.8g

Fiber: 1.7g

Peach Pie

Preparation Time: 40 MIN

Serving: 6

Ingredients:

- 2 cups almond flour
- 1 medium-sized peach, sliced
- ¼ cup raspberries
- 4 large eggs
- 6 tbsp. butter
- 2 tsp baking powder
- ½ tsp salt
- ¼ cup swerve
- ¼ tsp vanilla extract
- 2 tsp lemon zest

Directions:

1. Brush a 7-inches cake pan with oil and line with some parchment paper. Set aside.
2. In a medium-sized bowl, whisk together eggs and swerve. Set aside.
3. In another bowl, combine all the remaining dry ingredients and mix well. Slowly pour in the egg mixture, mixing constantly, and add the remaining

ingredients. Transfer to a mixing bowl and beat for 2 minutes on medium speed.
4. Pour the mixture into the prepared cake pan and shake a couple of times to flatten the surface. Wrap with some aluminum foil.
5. Plug in your instant pot and pour in 1 cup of water. Set the trivet at the bottom of the stainless steel insert and place the wrapped pan on top. Seal the lid and set the steam release handle to the 'Sealing' position.
6. Select the 'Manual' mode and set the timer for 25 minutes.
7. When done, perform a quick release by moving the pressure valve to the 'Venting' position.
8. Open the lid and remove the pan. Cool completely before serving.

Nutritional Values per serving:

Calories 221

Total Fats 19.4g

Net Carbs: 4.4g

Protein 6.6g

Fiber: 1.8g

Almond Butter Cookies

Preparation Time: 40 MIN

Serving: 15

Ingredients:

- 1 ½ cup almond flour
- ½ cup coconut flour
- 3 eggs
- ¾ cup coconut oil, melted
- 3 tbsp. almond butter
- ¼ cup cocoa powder, unsweetened
- ½ cup swerve
- ½ tsp salt

Directions:

1. Plug in your instant pot and pour in 1 cup of water. Set the trivet at the bottom of the stainless steel insert and set aside.
2. Line a round baking pan with some parchment paper and set aside.
3. In a large mixing bowl, combine together almond flour, coconut flour, cocoa butter, swerve, and salt. Add eggs, coconut oil, and almond butter. With a paddle attachment on, beat well on high speed until fully incorporated.

4. Scoop out 15 cookies and place them in the prepared baking pan. You will probably have to do this in several batches. Gently flatten each cookie with the palm of your hand and place the pan in your instant pot. Cover with aluminum foil.
5. Seal the lid and set the steam release handle. Press the 'Manual' button and set the timer for 25 minutes.
6. When done, release the pressure naturally for 15 minutes. Move the pressure handle to the 'Venting' position to release any remaining pressure.
7. Open the lid and remove the pan. Cool to a room temperature and then transfer the cookies to a wire rack to cool completely.

Nutritional Values per serving:

Calories 154

Total Fats 15.3g

Net Carbs: 1.5g

Protein 2.9g

Fiber: 1.9g

Mini Brownie Cakes

Preparation Time: 25 MIN

Serving: 4

Ingredients:

- 1 cup almond flour
- ½ cup cocoa powder, unsweetened
- ¼ cup swerve
- 4 eggs
- ¼ cup unsweetened dark chocolate, cut into chunks
- 1 tsp rum extract
- ½ cup coconut oil

Directions:

1. Plug in your instant pot and pour in 1 cup of water. Set the trivet at the bottom of the stainless steel insert and set aside.
2. In a large mixing bowl, combine together eggs, swerve, dark chocolate chunks, rum extract, and coconut oil. Mix well until light and creamy mixture. Sift almond flour and cocoa powder over the egg mixture and mix well again.
3. Divide the mixture between 4 ramekins and tightly wrap with aluminum foil. Place each ramekin on the trivet and seal the lid.

4. Set the steam release handle to the 'Sealing' position. Press the 'Manual' button and set the timer for 15 minutes.
5. When done, release the pressure naturally for another 15 minutes.
6. Open the lid and gently remove the ramekins using oven mitts. Place on a wire rack and cool completely before serving.

Nutritional Values per serving:

Calories 404

Total Fats 39.1g

Net Carbs: 4.8g

Protein 9.7g

Fiber: 4.7g

www.ingramcontent.com/pod-product-compliance
Lightning Source LLC
Chambersburg PA
CBHW071611080526
44588CB00010B/1100